KU-072-684

Blackburn
College

New Voices in Children's Literature Criticism

edited by

Sebastien Chapleau

First published 2004 by:

Pied Piper Publishing Ltd.
80 Birmingham Road
Shenstone
Lichfield
Staffordshire
WS14 0JU

Reprinted 2004, 2005

British Library Cataloguing in Publication
A catalogue record for this book is available from the British Library.

ISBN 0 9546384 4 1

Front cover design by Olivier Aubin

Printed in Great Britain by Bookchase (UK) Limited, Suite 9, Grove House, 320 Kensal Road, London, W10 5BZ, UK

To the contributors

Acknowledgments

I would like to express my deepest gratitude to those without whom the successful publication of this collection of essays would not have been possible. I would therefore like to thank the authors for their contribution to this project and for their remarkable interest, enthusiasm, and patience during the editing, evaluation, and production processes. I am more particularly grateful to Peter Hunt whose knowledge, passion, and support have been more than helpful, *once again*. I am also extremely grateful to Perry Nodelman who kindly agreed to write the preface to this collection.

I would also like to express my warmest gratitude to Rodolphe without whom doing all this would be quite insipid. It is your turn now *mon ami*.

Finally, I would like to extend my sympathy to all those who, like me, believe that engaging with the word and the world is worth the challenge.

Sebastien Chapleau, Cardiff, February 2004

For the critic, the important thing is the continuing transformation of reality, in behalf of the continuing humanisation of men (sic).

Paulo Freire

[I]t is important to keep in mind that the processes of reseeing, rethinking, and reconsidering our cultural and pedagogical assumptions need to be ongoing.

William J. Spurlin

[L]'écriture [...] vient donner la parole à celui qui, ne serait-ce qu'étymologiquement, ne peut parler. Entendons, celui qui ne peut parler la langue des adultes. Or, là est l'incontournable aporie: l'écriture, quant à elle, est toujours adulte, et c'est donc dans un a posteriori qu'elle trouve, de fait, son lieu. Ecrire sur l'enfance et l'enfance ne peut se faire qu'à distance, proprement d'en face, chaque mot couché sur le papier n'étant que l'aveu sans cesse renouvelé de la distance qui sépare l'ici d'un là.

Phillipe Romanski

Contents

Introduction

There exists a subject and an area of research that we've decided to call *Children's Literature* and which, I've always thought, sits at the crossroads of a wide variety of critical discourses. Most of us have read children's books when we were children, and most of us regard this experience as rather special. Who hasn't ever dreamt of being a prince, a princess, or maybe a magician? Who hasn't cried or laughed with their favourite fictional characters? Who hasn't wondered what it'd be like to fall down the rabbit-hole?

In our western societies, children's literature has acquired a somewhat mythological status. We see or hear references to children's books almost every day, almost everywhere. Yet, what *is* children's literature? Part of the answer is that the notion of Children's Literature is a *construct*, something that is given shape through various sets of interactions between a great variety of influencing parameters. But what *are* these parameters? All this, I believe, is fascinating. Fascinating but also frightening; maybe not for everybody, but at least for some researchers like myself, confronted with issues of definitions and critical perspectives. The question I keep asking myself isn't only *What is Children's Literature?*, but more precisely *What is Children's Literature and what does it signify?*.

This is the kind of questioning that has guided the authors of the essays collected here. As most of us will agree, a children's book is a book written by an adult for a child, *full stop*. But, and this is where and why I find it extremely *aporetic*, how are we supposed to approach this rather straightforward spectrum where an adult, a book, and a child are asked to meet *within* the space of a label: Children's Literature? To the question *What is Children's Literature?* we have an answer, but to the question *What does it signify?*, we seem to be left wondering. And with such wonderings, we seem to be going backwards. But isn't it what research is all about, going backwards? Beyond the rhetorical face of this epistemological question lie *essentially* problematic debates. As we engage in such debates, we get caught up in *polyphonic* arguments, polyphonic, but all guided by the same desire, the desire to analyse and, eventually, understand.

There is no such thing as the study of children's literature, Peter Hunt keeps insisting; there are only *approaches* to children's books. This is why this collection of essays reflects some of the aspects of the multifaceted essence of a subject the contributors and myself find so culturally/critically/politically complex: something we call *Children's Literature*.

Preface: 'There's Like No Books About Anything'

Perry Nodelman

Scholars who study nuclear physics or structural anthropology or Jacques Derrida tend to be admired by other people because they know things the other people do not know – and for that matter, may not even care to know. The more obscure and mysterious their knowledge, the more respect most people will have for it. If it seems obscure and difficult, then it must be wise and important. That might explain why specialists in children's literature tend to get so little respect. When it comes to children's literature, everyone's an expert. Everyone knows already.

Madonna, for instance, knows already. In an interview explaining why she decided to write some children's books, the pop star says: 'Now I'm starting to read to my son, but I couldn't believe how vapid and vacant and empty all the stories were ... There's like no books about anything.' Madonna is not alone in her conviction that she can characterise all children's books based on the few she has actually managed to read, or that she already knows exactly what kinds of book children should be reading. The students and parents I talk to about children's literature are almost always confident about these matters, long before I try to share my own expertise with them. They know that children have short attention spans, large imaginations, and a great need of moral improvement. They know that children's books are generally if not exclusively about princesses who live happily ever after, children who err and learn better, and adorable fuzzy animals in jackets and, sometimes, trousers. They already know everything there is to know about children and children's literature – and are surprised and a little offended by my suggestion that there might be more to know.

As the essays in this collection so interestingly reveal, there is, of course, a lot more to know. But I find myself wondering why so many people believe otherwise. And I find myself thinking that it has a lot to do with the very attitudes towards childhood that underpin the existence of children's literature in the first place.

Children's literature is centrally about not knowing. It came into existence when adults began to imagine childhood as a space necessarily separate from the world of adults, and separate because children needed to be kept from certain kinds of knowledge – to know less.

By definition, since then, childhood has been primarily a matter of *being* less: less experienced, less knowledgeable, less reasonable, less responsible, less capable. It is almost always defined in terms of its variation from what is taken to be its opposite – adulthood – and the variation is almost always a matter of lack. As a result, children's literature is that literature which lacks – lacks sexuality, say, or darkness, or complexity or big words – that literature which says less. Madonna can be certain that 'there's like no books about anything' because that's what most people believe children's books, by definition, are – book that are not significantly or deeply about anything, or at least about anything much. By definition, then, adults – all adults – simply in being adults, will always know more than children's literature can say. They will always possess an expertise that they will inevitably be assured children's literature cannot in itself possibly possess. How could they as adults not know more than children's literature does? And so what could experts in children's literature have to tell them? How could there possibly be more to know about that which itself knows and says so little?

Furthermore, if children's literature exists in order to allow children to know less, then children themselves are not capable of writing it. Its mere existence implies their innate lack of ability to do so – they lack the skill, the knowledge, the expertise. So it is adults who must provide children's literature for children, adults who must know what childhood is and who have the responsibility of revealing it to children in books that describe it. These adults must pretend to know less in order to show children the lesser world adults believe children know – or, more chillingly, hope to persuade children they know. At any rate, the childhood of children's literature is always a construct of adult imagining, a matter of adult expertise that expresses itself in the act of hiding itself – disappearing as adult expertise from the texts of children's literature in which it appears as a supposedly authentic vision of childhood. When it comes to children, indeed, it is the central responsibility of being adult to know all about childhood – to be expert about it. That is what childhood is – that which adults must know about because children themselves cannot.

Not surprisingly, the faith in adult expertise so inextricably interwoven into our most culturally powerful conceptions of childhood and children's literature must be blind to the possibility of a richer expertise – a greater knowledge than it is one's adult obligation to children to always have, a children's literature that says more or does more than one's own or at least the most common ideas of childhood suggest it must. As an intelligent and caring adult newly aware, as a parent, of her profound adult responsibilities towards children, Madonna can be certain that 'there's like no books about anything' – that no one before her will have ever had the guts or the vision to imagine a children's literature that transcended the common conventions of a lacking childhood.

In knowing that – and in deciding to do something about it herself – Madonna is not unlike many newcomers to children's literature – scholars as well as parents. In my career as an editor, a guest editor, and a referee for a number of children's literature journals, I have often found myself dealing with submissions by scholars from other literary fields who share Madonna's experience of reading a children's book to a child and developing a sudden awareness of expertise, scholars who seem then to say to themselves, 'Hey, I could write an article about this book! An academic article about children's literature – what a fresh and new idea!' The work they then produce and submit makes it clear that they had not even thought of doing the bibliographic searches to find previously existing scholarship they would have performed as a matter of course after choosing to write about any other kind of text. They clearly believe that, when it comes to children's literature, there's like no criticism about anything.

More depressing, I have often found myself as a referee and writer of book reviews pointing out all the previously existing critical work on the topics being discussed – work the writers of the work I am reviewing seem blithely ignorant of. There is something about children's literature – something about its connections with our ideas of childhood innocence – that invites even those who proclaim themselves its expert scholars to think of it as previously uncharted territory, a new found land they are the first ever to set foot on. It is up to each of us adults, it seems, to discover childhood anew and to imagine ourselves as its first saviours and civilisers.

I am happy to report that the new voices represented in this collection are not so innocent or ingenuous, and that they are deeply aware of the footprints left by those who walked that not-so newfound land before them. Indeed, what is most pleasurably new about these new voices is their awareness of and conversation with the old voices (including my own) – the way in which their placing of their work in the context of their predecessors makes it clear how very much a field of children's literature criticism does exist, how very much new expertise knows of, learns from, builds on and most significantly, challenges old expertise.

In his contribution to this collection, Peter Hunt, himself a wise old voice partaking in a new conversation, answers the criticism that the first edition of the overview of the field he edited, *The International Companion Encyclopedia of Children's Literature*, was uneven:

> It seemed to me that the *Encyclopedia* demonstrated an astonishing range of attitudes as well as an astonishing range of knowledge. To that critic who called it 'uneven', one can assume, 'even-ness', similarity of tone, of ideas, was desirable. I would say the reverse. Not only would uniformity be impossible to achieve, I would not wish to achieve it. What I would wish to achieve would be an acceptance that each style and each approach commands respect and pivots on the central author-book-reader negotiation.

To some extent, I agree. As the range of essays in this collection and the range of critical resources and theoretical perspectives they refer to and build on make clear, the presence of many voices is indeed a good thing, a multiplying of perspectives that can only enrich our knowledge of children's literature. But that can happen only if the many voices are listening to each other – if they are, in fact, having a conversation. Unfortunately, for all the value of their work that Hunt so rightly points to, the contributors to that first edition of the *Encyclopedia* – like so many other contributors and would-be contributors to our knowledge of children's literature, like the scholars unaware of previous scholarship in the field and like Madonna announcing the lack of children's books about anything – were not always doing that. As typical adult experts on children's literature, many of them seemed completely unaware than anyone else was even talking. And that is a shame.

It is a shame because we children's literature specialists really did need to be listening to each other. In suggesting that all these different styles and approaches command respect, Hunt implies that each adds a different component to our total knowledge of the field – something like the way in which Cardinal Newman, in his *Idea of a University*, imagined the disciplines each adding something unique to the totality of knowledge they all offered together, since '[a]ll that exists, as contemplated by the human mind, forms one large system' (1964: 33). But in fact, all the knowledge about children's literature represented in the *Encyclopedia* does not add up to one large coherent system. Rather than claiming separate parts of the total field, the different forms of expertise often offer competing visions of the same territory. What cognitive psychology has to tell us about childhood reading experience competes with what psychoanalysis or sociological theory have to say or what traditional humanistic literary scholarship simply assumes. They cannot all be right. Not acknowledging each other allows all of them to retain faith in their rightness – to blindly offer yet more versions of the ignorant expertise so aptly represented by Madonna.

We would all get further, I believe, if we paid attention to each other – if all of us experts in children and children's literature made ourselves aware of the ways in which we lay claim to the same territory in differing ways, if we listened to each others' differing versions of the same aspects of our field and took on the hard task of negotiating a place for our ideas that acknowledges and tries to account for their relationship to all the other ideas. The result of these sorts of engaged conversations would be anything but the kind of uniformity that Hunt quite rightly sees as undesirable. It would be a more complex and more complete vision of the complex way things are. It would alert us to the contradictions and complexities not only in our discourse about childhood and children's literature, but in childhood and children's literature themselves.

I suggested earlier that the contributors to this book are having conversations with their predecessors in the field of children's literature. It is true, nevertheless, that in writing about quite different aspects of the field, they tend to refer to different predecessors, different theories or bodies of knowledge, different forms of expertise. So the question remains: does this book represent the sort of complex discourse I have just been imagining? Are its contributors in conversation with each other?

In the most obvious way, of course, they are not. Having all written their pieces for the same deadline, each of them worked with a lack of awareness about what the others were doing. But in fact, a look at what they have produced as a whole reveals a complex conversation in progress – one that both continues and complicates discussion of some central threads in children's literature criticism.

Most central among those are the foundational binaries that I discussed earlier – the oppositions between child and adult, children's literature and adult expertise that underpin both the existence of a literature specifically for children and our ongoing adult interactions with it. In their purest form, these binaries represent impermeable borders – that which is childlike is by definition purely and absolutely non-adult – the opposite of adult – and so that which is children's literature is utterly devoid of – opposite to – the complexity, subtlety, and confusion of adult knowledge. But clearly, the separation of these presumed opposites is impossible. As well as being purely and blithely innocent of adult corruption (or purely and dangerously ignorant of adult wisdom), children are in the process of developing into adults – already always tainted, in being human, with the adult they are presumed to be opposite to. And children's literature, a product of adult expertise, always inevitably bears signs of the adult content it tries so desperately to deny and to hide. The binaries are not so opposite.

While they all do it differently, the essays in this collection all tend to disrupt the binaries - or to show how they are already disrupted. Laura Atkins speaks of a 'schism' in the goals of publishers of children's books caused by the contradictory constructions of childhood they try to maintain simultaneously. Katrien Vloeberghs describes how recent theories reveal the permeability of concepts of childhood, and Alison Waller how factual and fictional boundaries refuse to remain discrete in the discursive field of adolescence. In terms of reading children's literature, Virginie Douglas suggests that the novel she discusses questions 'the old adult/child dialectic' and David Rudd describes how the one he discusses 'troubles the adult-child binary.' Karen Sands-O'Connor asks for further trouble, inviting scholars 'to break out of rigid binary oppositions ... and begin instead to focus on plurality, both in literature's content and meaning.' Maiko Miyoshi focuses on plurality in suggesting that the writing by child characters represented within children's books 'makes everything, (including the existence of adult author, character in the texts, and the reader of the texts who receives such writing) variable, vague and uncertain.' Rebecca Rabinowitz extends the disruption and uncertainty to readers, recommending a focusing on 'the bits and pieces of queerness' – that which is supposed not to be there – that observant readers can find in children's books, and Vanessa Joosen suggests that the texts she discusses can encourage children to become observant readers themselves – to develop a theoretically impossible adult expertise in reading disruptively.

In dialogue with these writers describing the permeability of borders are others who contribute to the conversation by focusing on the way in which borders work to keep things in or out. Ann Alston describes how the safely enclosing homes so central to children's literature remains present as an implied ideal even in descriptions of less protective homes. Gabriele Thomson-Wohlgemuth shows how children's literature internationally is becoming more uniform, less disrupted by national variations, and Dominique Sandis postulates that children's literature evolves from international paradigms – boundaries that might work to control the expression of national difference.

In focusing on the question of borders and their disruptions, the contributors to this book offer an intriguing overview of the current state of our communal discourse about children's literature. They reveal two important things.

First, and most obviously, they reveal productive disruptions. As they work to reveal the permeability of the boundaries between child and adult, children's literature and adult expertise, they also disrupt the boundaries of the field of children's literature studies by showing how a wide range of other cultural and intellectual discourses might operate meaningfully within it. They reveal the abundant possibilities of an interdisciplinarity that reveals the limitations of the common adult assumptions about children's literature expertise and refuses to recognise academic borders.

But second, and perhaps less obviously: they reveal the significance of borders in the very act of insisting on their permeability. In her contribution to this book, Virginie Douglas suggests that the questioning of the conventional binaries 'may contribute, in future decades, to the dying out – or at least the absorption into mainstream literature – of the specific literary category called 'children's books." Personally, I doubt that will happen. As long as there are developmental theorists and graded schools and parents afraid to let their children use public transport, as long as there is a childhood of unknowing which invites adults to be protectors of and experts for children, as long as there are Madonnas around to assert that there are like no books about anything, there will be a children's literature – a literature that will declare the ways children are unlike adults and require both adults and children to become aware of the ways in which those categories do and do not operate in the lives of all of us. This book helps to create that awareness. It is a book that is like very much about something.

Bibliography

Hunt, Peter (ed.) (1996) *The International Companion Encyclopedia of Children's Literature.* 1st edition. London & New York: Routledge

'Madonna plans 'morality tale" in *BBC News World Edition*, 17 April, 2003. [http://news.bbc.co.uk/2/hi/entertainment/2955837.stm] (accessed 14/12/03)

Newman, John Henry (1964) *The Idea of a University*, Svaglic, Martin J. (ed.). New York: Holt Rinehart & Winston

The Knowledge: What Do You Need to Know to Know Children's Literature?

Peter Hunt

I conceive, therefore, as to the Business of being *Profound*, that it is with *Writers*, as with *Wells*; A Person with good Eyes may see to the Bottom of the deepest, provided any *Water* be there; and, that often, when there is nothing in the World at the Bottom, besides *Dryness* and *Dirt*, thou' it be but a Yard and a half under Ground, it shall pass, however, for wondrous *Deep*, upon no wiser a Reason than because it is wondrous *Dark*. (Swift, quoted in Harwood, 1995: 160)

Over the past thirty years, as 'Children's Literature' has gradually established itself as a subject of study in universities across the world, there has been a good deal of debate as to what it can or should constitute. You might object that it doesn't greatly matter: other disciplines, notably 'literature', get by without being defined very assiduously (Hunt, 2002). And yet, for me, the uneasy feeling persists that the texts (fiction, poetry and so on) that constitute 'children's literature' are merely visited or used by experts in other fields – theorists, or educationalists, or bibliographers – who could just as well be visiting some other body of texts. It is not that such peripatetic, marginal (and marginalized) discourses do not cohere into a discipline, for being a discipline should not be an end in itself. Rather, the texts and their situation seem to demand some kind of coherent response – a distinctive response that responds to their distinctiveness.

For the body of texts that is children's literature has two unarguable characteristics (however much they are ignored): the implied readers of the texts were/are 'children'; the actual users of the texts were/are predominantly 'children'. This seems to me to be the ineluctable, irreducible core of the texts of children's literature – and everything should feed into this, rather than taking from it. At the centre of its nature, children's literature is a negotiation (or a struggle) between author, material, and audience, a negotiation that is far more complex, more delicate and more extreme than the similar negotiations that go on (often unnoticed) where writers and readers are (supposedly) peers. All readers, as Valentine Cunningham put it, are bearers of:

> earlier knowledge and knowledges ... Reading is never innocent. It simply cannot exist unschooled. We are all taught to read, in the sense of grasping the mere [sic] mechanics of this doing; and then we're taught to read, to make sense of what we're 'reading', taught how to make meaning, to make sense of it. (2002: 5)

Children's literature operates at the point of learning mechanics and learning meaning – often simultaneously; the differences it makes to readers are, necessarily and logically, more intense. Consequently the locus of the study called Children's Literature must be the knowledge of, and the understanding of this negotiation, and in this chapter I would like to explore what this knowledge and understanding must entail.

Not unnaturally, such a fluid idea does not sit well in a world of specialisations, and it is often coupled with the idea that (ironically) Children's Literature is more properly a postgraduate rather than undergraduate study (students should progress before they regress). Thus we find ourselves producing Masters and Doctors of a subject (or of a small, specialised corner of it) who may not have the central tools of their trade.

The emergence of 'children's literature' has been greeted by a good deal of scepticism in traditional academia; even its supporters have had their doubts – for example, Vinnie Miner, Alison Lurie's Professor of Children's Literature in the novel *Foreign Affairs:*

> The very idea of making children's literature into a scholarly discipline, of forcing all that's most imaginative and free ... into a grid of solemn pedantry, pompous platitude, and dubious textual analysis – psychological, sociological, moral, linguistic, structural – such a process invites divine retribution ...
>
> Vinnie has a bad conscience about her profession. The success of children's literature as a field of study – her own success – has an unpleasant side to it. At times she feels as if she were employed in enclosing what was once open heath or common. First she helped to build a barbed-wire fence about the field; then she helped to pull apart the wildflowers that grow there in order to examine them scientifically. (1986: 235-6)

This conflict of interests is rooted in a very common conflict between the intellectual and the sentimental, which suggests – in a great many 'lay' readers of both children's literature and Children's Literature – a tacit suspicion of the analytical, amounting in many cases to anti-intellectualism. Inside academia there has been a great deal of unproductive negotiation between established academic disciplines, sometimes hinging on the relative status of, for example, education and literature departments, on the superiority of theory as against practice (or vice versa), or on the implication of the dominance of females in the field. The fact that Children's Literature now encompasses a bewildering range of subjects and approaches might suggest that it has no coherence; however, especially in the context of a fragmenting academic world, children's literature is no more incoherent than any other field or 'discipline'.

It may also be that the elements are particularly inchoate or incompatible. The negative situation is described by Rod McGillis:

> The rarefied theorising of the literary academic strikes the practising teacher as arid beyond tolerance, whereas the practical aims of the educationalist seem too limited and limiting to the theorist and historian of children's literature. The interest in bibliotherapy, sometimes expressed by the psychologically oriented critic ... is often dismissed as lacking the formalist rigor of serious literary analysis. And the interest in accumulating data, the purview of the librarian/media specialist, some [regard as] interesting but hardly intellectually stimulating or socially engaged. (1999: 203)

But this may only be the case because we do not usually place, for example, reviewing, pulp fiction, primary-school teaching and literary theory in the same category – but we do with Children's Literature (just as we do not, in the study of Literature, commonly acknowledge the audience, or acknowledge the negotiation described above).

This proximity of the elements of the study has been seen as both debilitating and humiliating. A few years ago, I was asked to contribute a book to a series of literary guides. The other books were to be on subjects like Modern Irish Poetry, and The Victorian Novel, or on authors such as Dante and Shakespeare. I was asked to contribute a volume that covered Children's Literature – that is, *all* children's literature: two hundred and fifty years in the western tradition, plus centuries of folk-tales, plus theory, applications, and detailed studies of major books. I pointed out to the publisher, with a certain lack of restraint, that this was ludicrous: why not volumes on Modern Irish Children's Poetry, the Victorian Children's Novel (several volumes on that), or Pullman or Mayne? Why should such a rich and influential heritage be treated as a sub-set of a sub-set? Is the subject – Children's Literature – to be marginalized into a single volume?

Well, needless to say, it was, but calmer thought suggested that there were at least two advantages to this. The first is that it was one *less* step on the road to the overproduction of academic and critical articles and books that has overwhelmed Literary Studies in general. As Wendell Harris pointed out, sardonically:

> If the only questionable result of the flood of publication ... were the difficulty of finding the grain amidst the chaff, it might be ungrateful to complain, especially if one were to take the excessively optimistic view that the amount of grain increases at the same rate as the chaff. ... The increase, one must recognise, is in no small measure the result of vita-dressing. ... What the ordinary intelligent ... academic

> must seek to stay in the game is the 'MPI', the minimal publishable idea, or ... the 'LPU', the least publishable unit. (1996: 213)

The second is that to bring many disparate ideas between one set of covers concentrates the mind towards synthesis, towards the (unfashionable) holistic. We force together what have been seen as polarities. Perhaps the most famous phrase in children's book 'theory' (one that never seems to disappear from its cyclical world) is the distinction – division – between 'book people' and 'child people' made by John Rowe Townsend in 1968. (Hunt 1990 62). This presaged a specialist world where it is quite possible to produce a journal called *Children's Literature* which makes no reference to children (Hunt, 1992: 1-2). At the other extreme might be Aidan Chambers's view in 1985:

> What ten years of teaching children's literature has taught me most clearly is that, so far as children and literature are concerned, the literature itself and critical approaches to it cannot be divorced from considerations of how the literature should be mediated to children. Put another way: *Any comprehensively useful criticism of children's literature must incorporate a critical exploration of the questions raised by the problem of helping children to read the literature* [italics sic]. (p123)

Such divisions (however benign in practise – and generally, the inhabitants of the world of Children's Literature see themselves as pleasant) could – should (and in Chambers's case do) – be resolved if the practitioners see themselves as part of the same project.

It is not simply the huge range of disciplines that have focused on children's literature that causes potential problems for an integrational model: it is that the way that people *think* in those disciplines is so different. What people think is worth saying about books, what they think is important or relevant or interesting, the assumptions they make about knowledge and quality of thought, and their modes of expression are often spectacularly at variance.

I am currently editing the second edition of the *Routledge International Companion Encyclopedia of Children's Books*, and among the 120 subjects discussed at length are: literature for disabled children, African oral culture, literary theory, storytelling, literacy, how picture books are perceived, the sociology of television, censorship, children and children's books as part of commercialised society, post colonialism, translation, and teaching – and surveys of children's books in almost every country in the world.

One of the critics of the first edition of the *Encyclopedia* described it as 'uneven'. In my view, that was totally inadequate as a description: it was very, very, very uneven in all possible ways! It seemed to me that the

Encyclopedia demonstrated an astonishing range of attitudes as well as an astonishing range of knowledge. To that critic who called it 'uneven', one can assume, 'even-ness', similarity of tone, of ideas, was desirable. I would say the reverse. Not only would uniformity be impossible to achieve, I would not wish to achieve it. What I would wish to achieve would be an acceptance that each style and each approach commands respect and pivots on the central author-book-reader negotiation.

Let me take five examples from the *Encyclopedia*, of the way writers write and think. The first is a writer whose target audience needs to know *about* poetry, rather than to examine it philosophically: the end result is transmission to children, rather than the understanding of literature as a mode of discourse. She is writing about A. A. Milne's poetry:

> What cannot be denied is that Milne has stood the test of time because the poetry *is* good. Years of writing for the magazine *Punch* trained a facility for well-crafted verse which Milne combined winningly with well-observed concerns of childhood. (1996: 201)

That is not the language of critical theory. It assumes that 'good' is mutually understood, that 'well-crafted' means the same thing, and that the definition of either would be fruitless. It assumes that knowledge about Milne's background is interesting and relevant, of itself, and is, by implication, unimpressed by critical schools that might suggest otherwise. It is friendly, accessible writing; it does not increase our understanding of *why* or *how* the poems are good – but in its context, it does not find it necessary to do so.

Here is a literary-critical theorist, discussing pictures in picture-books:

> The combination of two sign systems clearly provides a way of problematising the representational function of visual and verbal signs and of foregrounding the ways in which relations between signs and things are structured by culturally inscribed codes of representation and signification. (p400)

This is abstract in a quite different way; the implied reader has different preoccupations and is expected to understand more 'difficult' language, with many specialist words, addressing a difficult philosophical problem. The interest is a long way from 'simple' enjoyment of texts: the idea is to make what seems simple – looking at a picture-book – difficult, and there is a confident assumption that this is a natural process.

What do those writers have in common with an historian, probing the earliest children's books of all?

> The answer to the question, which children's texts are the oldest, depends on which civilisations achieved literacy first. The origins of literacy have long been the subject of debate, but the earliest attempts at writing that have been discovered so far, the marks on items intended for trade in the protoliterate period c. 4500 B.C., followed by cylinder seals that bear owners' marks and other identifiers, come from ancient Sumer, now the southern half of Iraq. Between 3000-2600 B.C., the Sumerians began writing on clay tablets ... (Hunt, 2004)

This is based on very specialist archaeological research, and is not in the least concerned whether anyone reads the texts, or how they are read or understood – and is definitely not concerned with living children and books.

At another extreme, here is a psychotherapist, writing about the *effect* of books – psychology and 'bibliotherapy':

> Not to be confused with 'therapeutic metaphor' is the development if so-called 'Narrative Therapy' (Epston and White, 1989). Originating as a variant of strategic family therapy, but employing Foucauldian notions about power, language and meaning, Narrative Therapy invites clients to become aware of how they have been participants in the construction of a 'dominant story' of their own life (for example, 'my life is a total failure') and instead to consider alternative ways in which they might have constructed their personal narratives. This encourages the noticing and valuing of instances when the person subverted or resisted the 'dominant story' – and the construction (for example) of an alternative self-narrative of success and 'heroic resistance' to perceived problematic influences. An example of the use of literary texts as an adjunct to such approaches can be found in Ridley (1999). (Hunt, 2004)

Note how, once again, we have a different language – a different preoccupation – and casual assumptions that we know about Foucault, and that we require scholarly references and would be prepared (or have the time) to read them.

Can we imagine that such a writer would be interested in an historical account of a specific country: for example:

> [t]he establishment of the Tokugawa government in 1603 marked the beginning of 250 years of peace, the Edo Era. It was also the starting point for books for children. In the middle of the seventeenth century, a few lesson books for children were published: the best of them was

> *Kin Mo Zui* (1666) by Tekisai Nakamura (1629-1702). (Hunt, 1996: 367)

And the answer to that last question must be yes. This is not a pious hope that all readers will, humanistically, be interested in all subjects, however remote from their central interests. Rather it is the recognition of a relationship, and respect for a different mindset – mutual respect often conspicuously lacking both within academia and between academia and the rest of the world. Book people and child people, whatever their 'expert' interests, occupy the same island.

In less poetic terms, if we want a new style of criticism and theory, then it must emanate *from* children's books (Hunt, 1994). Practitioners must know at least something of all of the elements of the negotiation. They must understand something of the historical and creative imperatives of writing and publishing; they must know the fundamentals of how books work and how readers read. Circling closely around these elements are ideology and cultural and literary history that infuse the production and reading of the book. This central star, as it were, can then support a solar system of specialists, whether they speculate on the philosophy of perception, or use the books to make the life of an individual more bearable.

And all of these negotiations and interactions must be *accessible*. A lot of writing about literature and (especially) theory in the last twenty years has seemed to operate on the devil's axiom that 'if you can say it simply, it can't be important'. As Frank Kermode said in 1989, the time 'is long past when the Common Reader could expect to follow the discourses of theoretical professors' (quoted in Harwood, 1995: 18) – which is a pity because they might have something that the untheoretical might find useful.

The Knowledge, then, which constitutes the True Study of children's literature, runs against the universalising, distinction-drawing, trends of literary and socio-cultural studies. We must bear in mind Raymond Tallis's maxim, that 'it is grand theorists, not common readers, who are *terribles simplificateurs*' (1995: 156). The central negotiation which is both children's literature and Children's Literature is essentially local and specific. Margaret Meek and Richard Flynn saw this in terms of:

> children's literature studies as a network of related scholarly, pedagogical and practical inquiries, all equal in status, their immediate importance depending on their usefulness in answering whatever question needs to be addressed at a particular point ... (Gannon, 2000: 38)

And, finally, we must invert – or continue to invert, the cultural neo-colonialism that, as Perry Nodelman famously put it 'judged audiences by the extent to which they were affected by books, so that, for instance, anyone who wasn't overwhelmed by Shakespeare was simply assumed to be an intransigent dummy', and rather, to make 'judgements of excellence in terms of the effects of books on their audience' (1985: 1-2).

Bibliography

Chambers, Aidan (1985) *Booktalk*. London: Bodley Head

Cunningham, Valentine (2002) *Reading After Theory*. Oxford: Blackwell

Gannon, Susan R. (2000) 'Children's Literature Studies in a New Century' in *Signal – Approaches to Children's Books 91*. Stroud: The Thimble Press, pp25-40

Harris, Wendell V. (1996) *Literary Meaning: Reclaiming the Study of Literature.* London: Macmillan

Harwood, John (1995) *Eliot to Derrida: The Poverty of Interpretation.* London: Macmillan

Hunt, Peter (1992) ''Tread Softly for you Tread on my Dreams': Academicising Arthur Ransome' in *International Review of Children's Literature and Librarianship,* 7(1), pp1-10

Hunt, Peter (1994) 'Criticism and Children's Literature: What Can We Say, and Who Wants to Listen?' in *International Review of Children's Literature and Librarianship,* 9(1), pp1-7

Hunt, Peter (ed.) (1996) *The International Companion Encyclopedia of Children's Literature.* London and New York: Routledge

Hunt, Peter (2001) *Children's Literature: A Guide.* Oxford: Blackwell

Hunt, Peter (2002) 'The Discipline of Children's Literature: To Benchmark or not to Benchmark?' in *Signal – Approaches to Children's Books* 99. Stroud: The Thimble Press, pp176-182

Hunt, Peter (ed.) (2004) *The International Companion Encyclopedia of Children's Literature.* 2nd edition. London & New York: Routledge

Lurie, Alison (1986) *Foreign Affairs.* London: Abacus/Sphere

McGillis, Roderick (1999) 'The Delights of Impossibility: No Children, No Books, Only Theory' in *Children's Literature Association Quarterly,* 23(4), pp202-208

Nodelman, Perry (ed.). (1985) *Touchstones: Reflections on the Best in Children's Literature Vol. 1.* West Lafayette, Indianna: Children's Literature Association

Tallis, Raymond. (1995) *Not Saussure. A Critique of Post-Saussurean Literary Theory*, 2nd edition. London: Macmillan

Townsend, John Rowe (1990) 'Standards of Criticism for Children's Literature' in *Children's Literature: the Development of Criticism*, Peter Hunt (ed.). London: Routledge, pp57-70

Messy New Freedoms: Queer Theory and Children's Literature

Rebecca Rabinowitz

> When we pick up complex things – like desire or gender – with primitive mental tools like binaries, we lose nuance and multiplicity.
> (Wilchins, 2002: 43)

Queer theory is a descendent of feminism and gay and lesbian theory and a recognisable child of deconstruction.[1] It is amazingly malleable, but it has clear goals: to seek out instability in traditional paradigms of sex (biology/anatomy), gender (social/cultural manifestations of sex), and sexuality (sexual orientation and desire) by finding gaps, holes, and inconsistencies of meaning. It addresses itself especially to binary systems, in which two categories are considered to be opposite and mutually exclusive, and also to be the only two categories that could ever possibly exist (homosexual/heterosexual, for example, or boy/girl). Rather than offering a stable new set of paradigms for sex, gender, and sexuality, queer theory looks at traditional categories and gleefully makes 'trouble' for them (Bornstein, 1994: 116; Butler, 1990: xxvii, 44; and Warner, 1992: 19). The trouble happens as 'the straight lines of all the binaries begin to unravel' (Merck, 1998: 4).

Queer theory shows sex, gender, and sexuality to be frequently fluid and dynamic. It explores:

> the open mesh of possibilities, gaps, overlaps, dissonances and resonances, lapses and excesses of meaning [that occurs] when the constituent elements of anyone's gender, of anyone's sexuality aren't made (or *can't be* made) to signify monolithically. (Sedgwick, 1993b: 8)

This 'open mesh' is not just theoretical; it is from real life. For a person's gender or sexuality not to 'signify monolithically' – in other words, not to have one unchangeable meaning, or not to follow a single, rigidly predetermined path – is common for both adults and children. But moments or lifetimes of such incongruity can lead to confusion and negative consequences, because we have little language and tolerance for them. Queerness works to expand what we think is possible and acceptable. It points out instability in the paradigms so that when such instability appears in people, as it inevitably does, it can be tolerated – or enjoyed.

Because 'queerness has been set up to challenge and break apart conventional categories, not to become one itself' (Doty, 1993: xv), no new definitions are formed in advance, nor are any formulas forced to work in all places. Instead, '[q]ueer commentary takes on varied shapes, risks, ambitions, and ambivalences in various contexts' (Berlant, 1995: 344). Depending on what it is analysing, queer theory finds all sorts of ways to unearth and explore places where binary models of sex, gender, and sexuality are inadequate or unstable. Queer theory addresses itself to books, paintings, films, and many other artistic and social phenomena. In literature studies, biological sex is rarely examined, because despite compelling theories about sex being at least partially socially constructed within the institutions of science and culture (see Harding, 1998; Holmes, 2000; Riley, 1988; and Stoltenberg, 1989), there are no physical bodies to study, so actual analysis cannot really take place. Literary gender and sexuality, however, are fully open to queer analysis. Under a queer lens, gender and sexuality reveal new aspects of characters, relationships, and literary themes. Fresh and spacious definitions of gender and sexuality make children's literature broader and deeper. They bring both new complexity and new clarification. They show that gender and sexuality, even in such a controlled world as children's literature, is complicated on the level that being human is complicated.

Some critics consider gender to be natural and inborn (essentialised) while other critics consider it socially constructed – but queer critics consider it *fluid*. Although many gender studies powerfully probe multiple literary messages about what it means to be each gender, both feminist analysis and new masculinity explorations (see Nodelman, 2002a, 2002b) often leave behind the space in between – the neithers, the boths, the incoherencies. Queer theory endows these spaces in between with significance. While other gender critics often take notice of characters with unusual gender or sexuality constructions, they consider them important specifically as exceptions. Queer critics use unusualness to show, instead of something about that particular character, that the very structures and definitions of gender and sexuality are rickety.

Since children's literature criticism is part of culture, it necessarily includes many institutionalised values as part of its discourse. Discourse dictates 'what is central and what is peripheral – what is a mistake, an anomaly, an accident, a joke. It tells us what to pay attention to and what to ignore' (Delany, 1999: 11). A queer approach to children's literature rethinks our discourse's common assumptions, reassessing the relative weight of myriad gender and sexuality markers. Markers previously tossed aside as exceptions or minutiae are newly analysed as indicative symbols. Suddenly, everything becomes queer. Queerness becomes not an exception but almost a rule, not unusual but wide and vast, lying not in any individual deviation but rather in the paradigms of gender and sexuality themselves.

Judith Butler's *Gender Trouble*, a founding text of queer theory, takes every gender signifier to be as important as every other. This is a new approach to gender markers, because traditional views of gender lean heavily on the idea of exceptions. If a male teenage character has a teddy bear, the bear is usually discounted as an exception to his other signifiers, which supposedly match his 'true' gender. His essential boyness itself is never questioned; no one suggests with any seriousness that he actually *is not* a boy (teasing excepted). Tomboyish girls and gentle boys are considered happy or unhappy deviations from supposedly clear categories of gender, the exceptions that prove the rule of binary gender.

Butler, however, counts all signifiers. She proposes a model of gender in which a person's gender signifiers are what *make* that person's gender, rather than coming *from* it. No particular marker either matches or does not match the person's 'essential' gender, because there is no gender without the symbols themselves: the signifiers combine in a package that actually *forms* the gender. In this model, gender is *performative.* Despite 'the illusion of an interior and organizing gender core' (1990: 173), Butler proposes that gender is made up of daily and lifelong actions, interactions, language, and rituals. 'Performance' doesn't mean theatrical performance; it means any aspect of a person that relates to gender in any way. Details from clothing to occupation to emotional habits to physical skills are all part of gender performance.

In suggesting that gender is performative, however, Butler never implies that it's simple to perform. First of all, little choice exists about whether to participate in the binary gender system. Opting out is sometimes possible partially, but never fully. A person or character becomes 'culturally intelligible as a human being only as they are assigned to one of two mutually exclusive categories' (Harding, 1998: 44); in other words, a role within a gender norm 'is necessary in order to qualify as a 'one'', a *person*, at all (Butler, 1993: 23). On top of that, society's fierce gender pressures make the question of agency – even about the tiniest actions – highly complex. Binary gender has such a huge 'web of expectations, rules, and demands' (Wilchins, 2002: 12) that transgender activist and theorist Kate Bornstein – while admitting that it's 'not a one-to-one correspondence' – likens it to a cult (1993: 103-106). Punishments for not adequately performing one's gender range from a strange invisibility, to 'giving up privilege' (Moraga, 2000: 75), to 'censure, ridicule, and danger' (Bornstein, 1994: 117).

But despite all the criteria measuring gender performance – or perhaps because there are so *many* criteria – every person has a different combination of signifiers, and therefore everyone's gender is different. Even in the controlled world of literature, each patchwork of signifiers is unique. Once gender is considered to be formed by patterns of signifiers, the two categories (clearly-definable male and clearly-definable female) disappear – or they become infinite. For example, cataloguing the gender signifiers of the four Tillerman children in Cynthia Voigt's *Homecoming* reveals four unique patchworks. Dicey Tillerman is a 13-year-old girl who is taken for a boy by about half the strangers she meets. Her signifiers come more from the male symbolic realm (a jack-knife, for example) than the female, but they refuse to add up to any classic gender archetype. Read performatively, Dicey simply has no place in a binary gender paradigm. She is traditionally interpreted as a tomboy, but the difference between Dicey and a tomboy, here, lies not in her character but in the way we read her. A queer reading allows her complexity; a binary reading stifles it. Her siblings are also unique patchworks. Sammy, for example, kicks and fistfights fiercely but is delighted to wear 'a costume with spangles on it' (Voigt, 1981: 238). Reading the Tillermans through binary gender is simply inadequate: it prevents their depth from showing.

Every gender patchwork, besides being unique, is also in constant flux because of the dynamic relationship between internal and external forces. In myriad and untraceable ways, gender identity is both *made* of the pressures and performances and also in ongoing negotiation with them. Creation and maintenance of self are dynamic and ongoing projects. Therefore, expecting people to fall easily and permanently into categories of male or female is like 'call[ing] a rainbow black and white' (Bornstein, 1994: 123). In this rainbow analogy, Bornstein is not simply adding in the colours between the binary's poles (which would only be shades of grey), but rather replacing the framework: rainbows do not include black and white at all. In binary gender, the perfect archetypal 'boy' and 'girl' are the black and white ends of the rainbow, which do not exist in a queer paradigm. There is no single marker that always and unquestioningly defines 'boy' or 'girl', so such a person or character cannot exist, even in theory.

Queer theory's project is to offer a new language in which gender's fluctuations, fluidity, and gaps are described as powerfully ambiguous and useful rather than simply ironic or unusual. Queer theory reads gender incoherency or inconsistency as natural and inevitable. This opens up the world of gender to include perhaps as many different genders as there are people. In literature, there are as many gender categories as there are characters. Or, because of the fluidity and shifting through time, as many genders as there are moments.

These rainbow-coloured genders then open up new levels of the texts in which they exist. The different gender patchworks in *Homecoming* enrich the overall theme of the quest for a home. Voigt sets up a sort of identity essentialism about her characters; each has a unique inner self that must be nourished. This identity essentialism then supports the variety of genders, working fascinatingly alongside the queerness of gender to create a text in which queerness itself becomes a naturalised part of humanistic notions of selfhood. Along with the bay and fresh vegetables and room to run, along with a new stability and permanence, the Tillermans' new home has space for their own personal and unique patchworks of gender. The place 'where the Tillermans could be themselves' (Voigt, 1981: 172) is under a queer lens.

Another thing queer theory can do is identify streams of meaning that contradict each other within the same book. Mapping the gender signifiers in Tamora Pierce's Song of the Lioness series reveals that the blatant feminist message is perched precariously: it leans simultaneously upon notions of essentialism *and* notions of performativity. A war exists at the series' very core about whether Alanna is a girl or a boy, whether gender is essential or performative, and whether selfhood is internal or dialectical. Song of the Lioness is a queer call to attention, proving gloriously how nothing can be proved. A queer lens reveals the series' various underlying discourses and their swirling relationships with each other, begging for readers educated in the slipperiness of gender and the problems of trying to contain it neatly.

Any reading strategy that opens up gender options 'without dictating which kinds of possibilities ought to be realized' (Butler, 1990: viii) counts as a queer approach, and the same is true for sexuality. Because the two are so intertwined, sometimes the question of *what* exactly is being blurred is a question in itself. For example, when a man named George, happening to be unclothed, finds out that his young male friend training for knighthood is actually a young girl living in drag, he makes her turn away until he can find his breeches; 'she obeyed, [but] arguing, "That's silly. I've seen you naked before"' (Pierce, 1983: 134). She *has?* The fact that Alanna has seen George naked before is shocking to the reader – how could this happen without our knowledge? Does this prove her point – the insignificance of the moment – or does it open up whole new categories of possibilities? Are the possibilities about gender or sexuality? Or both? The earlier (unseen) scene places her in a male position, because traditionally only a male can see another male naked without warranting attention. Does this mean Alanna is sort of a boy? And what does that mean for the potential sexuality implied by the need to turn away? Pondering these questions, or any that come from this type of gap or ambiguity of meaning, is a queer endeavour.

Sexuality might not have as obviously a prominent role in children's literature as gender, but its place is quite significant. Various textual configurations and assumptions – in picture books as well as young adult books – work to follow a hegemonic discourse of sexuality. The fiercest flow, of course, is in the direction of heterosexual imperatives. Sometimes those imperatives aren't absolute, and gay characters are included, along with the general notion that gay people exist. And sometimes there is queerness where it is least expected. In order to fully recognise the levels of complex sexuality already existing in texts, our reading strategies need to be queered. Queer theory can help open up ways of looking at sexuality in children's literature without panicking, and also without treating children as adults.

Queer theory sees sexuality in children's literature even when it does not take the form of sexual feelings or acts. Take, for example, the sailboat scenes in Voigt's *Homecoming*, where queerness manifests itself not in same-sex attraction but in sexuality that cannot be easily categorised and that exists beyond concrete sexual events or easily-labelled desires. Two boys who 'wore only bathing suits' (p190) spray each other with a hose, splashing Dicey. For the next eighteen pages (pp190-207), symbols of sex abound. There are sails that are stiff and then go limp. Dicey closes her eyes, rocking with the boat and wishing 'she could stop breathing and give herself entirely over to the movement and the being still' (p202). After a while, '[t]he sun beat down hotter, and her skin started to run with sweat' (p203); she finds herself 'sticky [and] uncomfortable' and finds the sails, previously full, to have fallen 'lifeless and quiet, flapping morosely' (p203).

A Freudian reading of these symbols would conclude that Dicey has sex, either several times or in a temporally rearranged way, in this scene. Because Jerry owns the boat and teaches her to sail and is a boy, and because his smile 'tease[s] her' (p205), the conclusion would be that Jerry is the person she has sex with. But queer readings look more broadly and allow sexuality to be both deeper and less definite. First of all, no matter what happens between Dicey and Jerry, several textual details imply that Jerry and Tom are a couple. But where does that leave Dicey? One queer way to look at the scene is that Dicey has sex with a gay or bisexual boy. Another is that all three of them have sex, since Tom is sailing the boat too. A third is that Dicey, in some way, has sex with the sailboat. In a Freudian or literal reading, this would, of course, sound absurd; but one of the unique things about queer criticism is that it allows sexuality to *exist* without necessarily forcing it onto the level of the literal. It allows Dicey's sailing experience to be part of her own sexuality, without dictating exactly how – and without any act of sex.

Sedgwick writes about 'silent presumptions ... that are true only to varying degrees, and for many people not true at all: that everyone 'has a sexuality,' for instance, and that it is implicated with each person's sense of overall identity in similar ways ....' (1993b: 8). Queer theory reaches beyond these presumptions to shine light on little, big, casual, deep, and dynamic bits of sexuality that don't necessarily correspond with binary sexual identities – or quantifiable sexual identities at all. What does it mean if a person, or two people, sneak up to a Rembrandt painting in a museum and kiss it (Chambers, 1999: 86-87, 272-274)? What does it mean if the man in that painting startlingly resembles one of the book's characters (p58, p80, p86, p88)? Are the possibilities queerer from being in the same book as other, more blatant queerness (including bisexuality, a character who refuses a label, and the mistaken gender identity of a very femme man)?

Even biological sex, though hard to deconstruct without actual bodies to analyse, can be analysed in literature on rare occasions. Stereotypical discourse constructs female sexuality as passive or receptive, male sexuality as active or assertive; these notions colour even portrayals of physiology. But in Garret Freymann-Weyr's *My Heartbeat*, for example, Ellen wonders 'what makes the body – mine and his – tremble, leak, and break open?' (2002: 135-6). From a queer perspective, this is groundbreaking just for implying that male and female sexual response have more in common than in contrast. The characters' humanity – which, here, is their physiology – ranks higher than the binary.

It is high time for queerness to have a larger place in children's literature. It allows both characters and readers a richer and fuller humanity. More gay, lesbian, bisexual, and transgendered characters are long overdue; femme boys, butch girls, and all sorts of queer folks belong in children's literature fully as much as they belong in the rest of literature and art. But creating them is a job for fiction writers, not critics. Queer critics aim to find the bits and pieces of queerness that exist already, that *insist* on sprouting in books of all kinds, irrespective of author intention. Subversiveness and hegemony – queerness and normativeness – occur in all sorts of different relations to each other. They can be side by side, at war or at peace, checkerboarded, quilted, or interwoven. '[B]asically heterocentrist texts can contain queer elements', and 'the queer often operates within the nonqueer, as the nonqueer does within the queer' (Doty, 1993: 3). Resistance is mobile, dynamic, and sly. This is why determining relative queerness – ranking it – is only one type of queer project, not the only one. Most books turn out to be, as Sedgwick says of most gender performances, 'kinda subversive, kinda hegemonic' (1993a: 15). But queerness can be found all over. Not every book will yield the same amount or type, but almost every book will yield something.

There is room among queer critics for child readers. Adapted variously according to the age of the child, queer theory can help child readers develop their own critical awareness and actively form their own opinions and reading strategies. This can add extra layers and richness to their reading experiences, allowing gender and sexuality as much complexity in literature that child readers will realise, as they grow, exists in real life. The fluidity of gender and sexuality that exists in children's literature is about the nature of humanity, not an assumed unformedness of people who are young. Queer theory provides room and language to help both adult and child readers explore 'messy new identities we don't like and can't name that create possibilities and freedoms we never intended' (Wilchins, 2002: 295). The freedoms apply to longings we already have and longings we do not have yet; selves we cherish and selves we do not understand; identities we are punished for and identities that are yet invisible. Queer theory can stretch as far as our own minds will let it.

Bibliography

Berlant, Lauren & Warner, Michael (1995) 'What Does Queer Theory Teach Us About *X*?' in *PMLA,* 110, pp343-349

Boone, Joseph A, et al. (eds.) (2000) *Queer Frontiers: Millennial Geographies, Genders, and Generations.* Madison, Wisconsin: University of Wisconsin Press

Bornstein, Kate (1994) *Gender Outlaw: On Men, Women, and the Rest of Us.* New York: Vintage

Butler, Judith (1990) *Gender Trouble.* New York: Routledge

Butler, Judith (1993) 'Critically Queer' in *GLQ,* 1, pp17-32

Chambers, Aidan (1999) *Postcards from No Man's Land.* New York: Dutton

Delany, Samuel R. (1999) *Shorter Views: Queer Thoughts and the Politics of the Paraliterary.* Hanover, New Hampshire|: Wesleyan University Press

Doty, Alexander (1993) *Making Things Perfectly Queer: Interpreting Mass Culture.* Minneapolis: University of Minnesota Press

Freymann-Weyr, Garret (2002) *My Heartbeat.* Boston: Houghton Mifflin

Harding, Jennifer (1998) *Sex Acts: Practices of Femininity and Masculinity.* London: Sage

Holmes, Morgan (2000) 'Queer Cut Bodies' in *Queer Frontiers: Millennial Geographies, Genders, and Generations*, Joseph A. Boone, et al. (eds.). Madison, Wisconsin: University of Wisconsin Press, pp84-110

Merck, Mandy, Segal, Naomi & Wright, Elizabeth (eds.) (1998) *Coming Out of Feminism?* Oxford: Blackwell

Moraga, Cherrie, with Witherspoon, Rosemary (2000) 'An Interview with Cherrie Moraga: Queer Reservations; or, Art, Identity, and Politics in the 1990s' in *Queer Frontiers: Millennial Geographies, Genders, and Generations*, Joseph A. Boone, et al. (eds.). Madison, Winconsin: University of Wisconsin Press, pp64-83

Nodelman, Perry (2002a) 'Making Boys Appear: The Masculinity of Children's Fiction' in *Ways of Being Male: Representing Masculinities in Children's Literature and Film*, John Stephens (ed.). New York: Routledge, pp1-14

Nodelman, Perry (2002b) 'Who the Boys Are: Thinking About Masculinity in Children's Fiction' in *New Advocate,* 15, 1, pp9-18

Pierce, Tamora (1983) *Alanna: the First Adventure.* New York: Random House

Pierce, Tamora (1984) *In the Hand of the Goddess.* New York: Random House

Pierce, Tamora (1986) *The Woman Who Rides Like a Man.* New York: Random House

Pierce, Tamora (1988) *Lioness Rampant.* New York: Random House

Rabinowitz, Rebecca (2002) 'Both, Neither, Nor, More: Queer and Nonbinary Gender in Children's Literature.' MA thesis. Simmons College. [Available at: http://www.suberic.net/~rcwr/thesis.html]

Riley, Denise (1988) *'Am I That Name?' Feminism and the Category of 'Women' in History.* Minneapolis: University of Minnesota Press

Sedgwick, Eve Kosofsky. (1993a) 'Queer Performativity' in *GLQ* 1, pp1-16

Sedgwick, Eve Kosofsky. (1993b) *Tendencies.* Durham, North Carolina: Duke University Press

Stoltenberg, John (1989) *Refusing To Be a Man: Essays on Sex and Justice.* New York: Meridian, pp25-39

Voigt, Cynthia (1981) *Homecoming.* New York: Fawcett Juniper

Warner, Michael (1992) 'From Queer to Eternity: an Army of Theorists Cannot Fail' in *Voice Literary Supplement*, June, pp18-19

Wilchins, Riki (2002) 'A Continuous Nonverbal Communication', 'Deconstructing Trans', 'Queerer Bodies' in *Genderqueer: Voices From Beyond the Sexual Binary*, Joan Nestle, Clare Howell, Riki Wilchins (eds.). Los Angeles: Alyson, pp11-17, 33-46, 55-63

Notes

Much thanks to Susan Bloom, Kristion Cashore, Deborah Kaplan, Cathryn Mercier, Perry Nodelman and Dylan Ward.

The Apple That Was Not Poisoned: Intertextuality in Feminist Fairytale Adaptations

Vanessa Joosen

Ever since children's literature gained its status as a part of literature worthy of academic study, children's texts have received much attention from scholars and critics. One of the most frequently studied genres is the fairy tale, especially the tales that were collected by Charles Perrault and the Grimm Brothers. 'Adult' literary theories such as feminist, Marxist and psychoanalytical theories have provided new perspectives on the tales. At the same time there has been a lively interest in fairy tales on the part of writers, who invent new tales or rewrite older ones. Authors who compose their own versions of traditional tales do not write in a vacuum. They may be well aware of the criticism that has led to new perspectives on the tales, even if they have not read specific critical texts. It is impossible to imagine contemporary society and literature without the influence of feminism, Marxism or psychoanalysis, which have shaped the spirit of our age to such an extent that writers and illustrators are inevitably influenced by them.

In this essay, I will investigate the relationship between the theoretical feminist discussion on fairy tales and fictional adaptations of the same stories. In some fairy tale retellings, the impact of feminism is noticeable when the author tries to be 'politically correct'. In other adaptations, writers overtly refer to critical texts, so that the literary theory becomes an intertextual link in its own right. I will mainly focus on two feminist retellings that are (partly) based on 'Snow White'. In the first part I will discuss a tale with an explicit political agenda, an adaptation that openly refers to a corpus of feminist fairy-tale theory. This is Linda Kavanagh's 'The Princesses' Forum', the opening chapter of a collection of feminist retellings, titled *Rapunzel's Revenge*. In the second part I will look at Emma Donoghue's 'The Tale of the Apple' (1985), which appeared in *Kissing the Witch* (1997) and which deals with issues similar to those in *Rapunzel's Revenge*, but offers a more creative solution to feminist issues.

Fairy tales for feminists: the princesses' agenda

Feminism has been, and still is, without a doubt, one of the most powerful critical apparatus to influence fairy-tale retellings. Many contemporary adaptations are not only written by women, they also revise gender roles and give women a more active part to play. In Catherine Storr's *Clever Polly and the Stupid Wolf* (1995), for instance, the protagonist is an intelligent young girl who reverses the traditional fairy-tale pattern by tricking and teasing the wolf. Some contemporary fairy-tale retellings are constructed with an overt feminist message, and the subtitle of *Rapunzel's Revenge, Fairytales for Feminists*, leaves no questions about its political agenda.

In 'Feminist Fairy-Tale Scholarship' (2000), Donald Haase sketches out the most important tendencies in the way some feminists have dealt with fairy tales, ranging from anthologies and revisionist adaptations to studies on the Grimms' editing practices and the reception of the tales. Many of the issues in Haase's article are explicitly and implicitly addressed in *Rapunzel's Revenge*, especially in Kavanagh's opening chapter, 'The Princesses' Forum (PP5-11). Written in 1985, this introductory tale both refers to issues that feminists had dealt with earlier, and at the same time anticipates tendencies that became important in a later stage of feminist fairy-tale scholarship.

One of the first issues raised by feminist critics was the lack of positive, active roles for women in the best-known tales. In the 1970s and early 1980s fairy-tale scholars such as Sandra Gilbert, Susan Gubar, Andrea Dworkin and Karen Rowe focussed on the forces limiting female characters to negative or stereotypical images and idealised romantic futures (Haase, 2000: 16-21). *Rapunzel's Revenge* explicitly and implicitly places itself along the line of those critics – explicitly in the introduction, 'The Princesses' Forum', where some female fairy-tale protagonists discuss their portrayal in the tales, and implicitly by reversing gender roles in the various adapted tales. According to Dworkin, the Grimm tales picture women invariably as 'wicked, beautiful, and passive, while portraying men, in absolute contrast, as good, active and heroic' (Haase 17). In *Rapunzel's Revenge* this image is explicitly corrected: Sleeping Beauty is 'really quite wide awake', Cinderella calls herself a 'self-respecting woman' and Little Red Riding Hood complains that they are 'all the victims of stereotyping' (pp5-6). The princes, on the other hand, are 'tired of always feeling under pressure to be brave and fearless' (p9).

Two critics who were vital in recognising female stereotyping in literature were Sandra Gilbert and Susan Gubar. They devoted part of their feminist milestone, *The Madwoman in the Attic* (1979), to a discussion of 'Snow White' and argued that the tale presents two negative stereotypes of women, the innocent passive Snow White and the evil jealous stepmother. Both roles are imposed on women by patriarchy, which in the tale is symbolised by the voice in the mirror. The prologue of *Rapunzel's Revenge* takes on many of the thoughts formulated in *The Madwoman in the Attic*, as becomes clear in the following comparison:

Gilbert and Gubar	Kavanagh
Snow White has become an idealised image of herself, ... and as such she has definitively proven herself to be patriarchy's ideal woman, the perfect candidate for Queen. (p41)	'I'm tired of having to behave as princesses are supposed to behave,' said Snow White. (p6)
[In] her absolute chastity, her frozen innocence, her sweet nullity, Snow White represents precisely the ideal of 'contemplative purity' ... Snow White is not only a child but ... childlike, docile, submissive. (p39)	'I'm not delicate, I'm not silly and I'm certainly not weak.' (p6)
[The] tale concentrates on the conflict in the mirror between mother and daughter, woman and woman, self and self. (p37)	'[I]n many of our stories, our enemies are other women.' (pp7-8) 'The first change *I* want to make,' said Snow White, 'is to get my stepmother the Queen on our side.' (p8)
[The] patriarchal voice of judgement [rules] the Queen's – and every woman's – self-evaluation. (p38) [F]emale bonding is extraordinarily difficult in patriarchy: women almost inevitably turn against women because the voice of the looking glass sets them against each other. (p38)	'Once we're not in competition for men's approval, it won't matter which of us is better-looking. Then she'll have no reason to be jealous with me anymore.' (p8) '[T]here will be no need for other women to be our enemies if we're not fighting over who gets those macho idiots.' (p8)
[T]he Queen [is] a woman of almost infinitive creative energy, witty, wily, and self-absorbed as all artists traditionally are. (p39)	'Besides [my stepmother is] a very brilliant woman, with her own laboratories downstairs in the castle dungeon. I'm sure I could convince her to develop the science of pharmacology for good rather than evil.' (p8)

With this comparison it is not my aim to prove that Kavanagh read Gilbert and Gubar and based her own story on that text, although *The Madwoman in the Attic* is such a milestone that every self-respecting feminist probably *has* read it. However, I do argue that Gilbert and Gubar's discussion of 'Snow White' can be considered to be a key-text that both reflected and influenced feminist thinking about fairy tales in the 1970s and 1980s, and that *Rapunzel's Revenge* incorporates these ideas as well. Both texts are part of a larger intertextual corpus of feminist thinking.

From the 1970s onwards, critics such as Marina Warner and Ruth Bottigheimer started concentrating on the editing practices of the Grimm Brothers, and found that their revisions were often an ideological 'inscription of patriarchal values' (Haase, 2000: 27) that had a negative effect on the portrayal of women in the tales. Bottigheimer, for instance, studied the evolution of 'Our Lady's Child' in the Grimms' different editions, which led to the following conclusion:

> Between 1807 and 1812, the tale underwent considerable change. The plot remained constant, but shifts in vocabulary and motivation depersonalized the heroine and intensified her suffering and isolation. The consistent direction of editorial change [indicates] a well-honed gender-differentiated design for substituting compliant for obstinate behaviour in [Wilhelm Grimm's] young female readership. (1987: 87)

Written in the 1980s, when these discussions were going on, 'The Princesses' Forum' (Kavanagh, 1985) also refers to the editing practices of the Grimm Brothers. When Sleeping Beauty complains that in many stories women are enemies, Cinderella aligns herself with Bottigheimer's theory: 'That's because men wrote the stories ... It makes them feel good to have women fighting among themselves for male attention.' (p8)

As a reaction to this limitation of female roles, some critics, such as Karen Rowe, stressed the woman's voice in the tales. In her 1986 essay, 'To Spin a Yarn', Rowe argued that the stories were told with a double addressee in mind:

> in the history of folktale and fairy tale, women as storytellers have woven or spun their yarns, speaking at one level to a total culture, but at another to a sisterhood of readers who will understand the hidden language, the secret revelations of the tale. (p301)

For the storytellers and their female audience the tales thus function as a way to covertly pass on secret information. Even though *Rapunzel's Revenge* was written before Rowe's essay was published, the prologue already anticipates the idea of the double addressee. When the princesses think that Rapunzel is pregnant, Cinderella immediately knows where to go, namely to Red Riding Hood's grandmother: 'She's an expert in dealing with this kind of situation.' (p6) In this story the princesses do in practice what Rowe described in theory: they pass on information about female problems such as unwanted pregnancy without explicitly saying what they mean: Cinderella does not mention 'abortion' so that only a knowing addressee will understand. This implicit function of the tales creates a special tie between female storytellers and listeners. Feminists have more than once stressed the importance of female bonding, and so does Kavanagh. The princesses feel no longer dependent on men, now that they can rely on each other. Rapunzel says the other women have rescued her (p6), whilst Snow White wants to involve her stepmother (p8) in the women's movement.

Whereas critical theory has often signalled problematic issues in the Grimm tales, the retellings usually go one step further and try to offer an alternative to the stereotypical portrayal of women. The reversal of gender roles and the abandonment of forces limiting women were some of the issues concerning emancipatory feminism. Undoubtedly, this movement has contributed largely to the liberation of women, enabling them to take on new professions, to vote, to raise their voices, to write. On the other hand, the danger of this kind of feminism is that it may produce new stereotypes. And since *Rapunzel's Revenge* was written with an overt emancipatory agenda, it also displays some of the problems this movement had to cope with. Paradoxically, the story is implicitly based on the same stereotypes it explicitly challenges. The prejudice that most princesses lack intelligence is a good example. When Rapunzel complains she has put on weight and feels sick in the morning since the prince visited her, all the princesses fear she is pregnant. She herself says all this in 'happy innocence', is 'bewildered at the response' and even makes 'a mental note to keep quiet in future', which she then forgets (pp5-6). Although it turns out that the pill caused all symptoms, the misunderstanding shows that Rapunzel is not too bright. At the same time, the incident confirms the stereotype of bossy, quarrelling women. One of the main goals of feminism is to give women a voice, but Rapunzel is snapped at so that she decides to keep quiet. When she does make a remark, Cinderella says: 'If I were you ... I'd keep my mouth shut.' (p6)

Another issue which the princesses fail to correct is their relationship with men. Although they claim that they have had enough of princes who have foot fetishes (Cinderella) and are too stupid to find a ladder (Rapunzel), they cannot do without them. Red Riding Hood blushes at the recent memory of the woodcutter (p6), and as soon as a few princes arrive, the women only focus on them. Eventually each princess leaves with her new lover and the female gathering breaks up. The only person to stay behind is Snow White, who goes to her stepmother's laboratory and is thus is the only woman who really makes an effort towards female bonding. This is also the theme of the story that I will discuss in the next section, 'The Tale of the Apple' (Donoghue, 1997).

Kissing the witch

Emma Donoghue's *Kissing the Witch* (pp43-58) is a fairy-tale collection that 'disrupts the usual patterns of heterosexual desire' (Harries, 2000: 134) and provides in practice what some feminist/lesbian critics described as a lack in fairy tales: female bonding. All but one of the stories retell well known fairy tales, with an emphasis on the love between women or with a psychological explanation for troubled female relationships. In these tales, Donoghue takes on many of the issues formulated by feminist scholars, such as Gilbert and Gubar and Marina Warner, and can thus be intertextually linked to feminist criticism. But, in contrast to *Rapunzel's Revenge*, Donoghue takes the discussion a step further and writes about her own positive alternative to patriarchy, namely the love that can exist between women.

In Donoghue's retelling of 'Snow White', 'The Tale of the Apple', four women are central: Snow White (in this tale a nameless girl), her mother, her nurse and her stepmother. Their struggles form the core of the tale, although the plot is also driven by Snow White's father and to a lesser extent by the seven woodsmen (replacing the seven dwarfs). In this respect, the tale draws further on what Gilbert and Gubar (1979: 36) identified as the central action of the tale: the relationship between Snow White and her stepmother as the representations of the angelic and the monster female type.

Before the stepmother arrives, another woman is present in the margins of the tale: Snow White's biological mother. In the Grimm version, she lacks psychological background and is merely pictured as a woman longing for a child. Like many retellings, 'The Tale of the Apple' adds characters' private thoughts and anxieties, and in these extensions, some of Gilbert and Gubar's ideas are reflected. They have addressed, for instance, the lack of a role-model for Snow White: the girl's future role as a queen threatens to become another prison, from which her only escape are the badness and plots that her stepmother taught her (p37). In Donoghue's tale, Snow White's mother, who is painfully aware of every queen's tragic fate, asks herself: 'The daughter I carry will have hair as black as ebony, lips as red as blood, skin as white as snow. What will she have that will save her from my fate?' (p44)

Gilbert and Gubar identified the main patriarchal voice in this tale as the mirror's. Again Donoghue follows in their footsteps. After Snow White's initial prejudices against her young stepmother, a friendship starts to develop. This first effort towards female bonding is disrupted when the King, who is also the patriarch, carelessly asks: 'But which of you is the fairest of them all?' (p47), an echo of the stepmother's dialogue with the mirror. The women's laughter sounds 'a little out of tune' and their rivalry takes a new turn: 'our eyes were like mirrors set opposite each other.' (p48)

In 'The Tale of the Apple', Snow White's father already upsets her before he remarries, and their play is heavily sexually loaded. It is suggested that the King is well aware of his incestuous feelings, as he takes on a new wife when Snow White starts menstruating, leaving the young girl confused (p47). This explains why she feels threatened by her stepmother, and fails to see that this insecure young woman could be an ally. Indirectly, fairy tales are blamed for Snow White's distrust of women as well: 'I knew from the songs that a stepmother's smile is like a snake's, so I shut my mind to her from that very first day.' (p46) In this quotation, the songs shape Snow White's image of 'the stepmother', in a way that the Grimm tales have for many children. If the girl had been provided with more positive images of women, she may have given her stepmother a chance. This idea is also present in Warner's *From the Beast to the Blonde*, where she pleads for a rehabilitation of the stepmother:

> As remarriage becomes more and more common, stepmothers find they are tackling a hard crust of bigotry set in the minds of their new children, and refreshed by endless returns of the wicked stepmother in the literature of childhood. (1994: 237)

Snow White cannot see that her stepmother is a victim of patriarchy herself. When the King's new wife cannot get pregnant and is incapable of reproducing the next patriarch, she is locked up and treated with inhumane medicines (Donoghue, 1997: 48-49). Instead of becoming allies, the two women turn against each other and when her father dies, Snow White flees. The seven woodsmen who adopt her further contribute to her distrust. Although during the stepmother's three visits there is no indication that she wants to harm Snow White, the princess is each time left so devastated that the woodsmen blame the queen and ascribe evil powers to her.

The strength of Donoghue's retelling is that she not only takes on issues addressed by feminist and lesbian critics, but also provides the reader with a positive alternative to the patriarchal view of women. One way of doing this is by reinterpreting the central symbols of the tale, such as the mirror and the apple. In the Grimms' version of 'Snow White', the apple can be read as symbolising absolute hatred between women. In 'The Tale of the Apple', however, the apple becomes the exact opposite: a token of reconciliation and love. In this story, the first apple of the year is given as a privilege and symbol of affection, so that when the queen offers this fruit to Snow White, she is not trying to poison her but to show her respect. The fact that this symbol of love is mentioned in the title shows how important this new symbolic meaning is to the rest of the story. Eventually Snow White bites the apple and realises it is not poisoned. She is not saved by a prince, because there is nothing to be saved from. Once the patriarch has died and the mirrors are broken (p55), the young girl overcomes her prejudices and opens up to female bonding. Snow White returns to her stepmother and lives happily ever after.

Conclusion

There has been one absentee in this article that I wish to include in this final paragraph: the child or adolescent reader. Children do not have access to literary criticism and are therefore unable to obtain full understanding of the theoretical intertexts that are referred to in some fairy-tale adaptations. Nevertheless, these retellings can provide an enriching experience in the development of young readers. In showing children a new perspective on stories they already know, these 'alternative' fairy tales can give young readers a first impression of what critical theory can bring about: children who make the connection with the original tales may become aware of gender-issues in these texts which they had not noticed before, and this experience may lead to a greater awareness when they read similar stories in the future. These revisions bring about in young readers an awareness not only of other texts, but also, most importantly, of their own reading processes. Retelling then not only implies rereading, but most importantly, rethinking.

Bibliography

Bacchilega, Cristina (1997) *Postmodern Fairy Tales: Gender and Narrative Strategies*. Philadelphia: University of Pennsylvania Press

Bottigheimer, Ruth B. (1987) *Grimms' Bad Girls and Bold Boys: The Moral and Social Vision of the Tales*. New Haven: Yale University Press

Donoghue, Emma (1997) *Kissing the Witch: Old Tales in New Skins*. New York: HarperCollins Publishers

Gilbert, Sandra M. & Susan Gubar (1979) *The Madwoman in the Attic: The Woman Writer and the Nineteenth-Century Literary Imagination*. New Haven: Yale University Press

Haase, Donald (2000) 'Feminist Fairy-Tale Scholarship: A Critical Survey and Bibliography' in *Marvels and Tales,* 14, 1, pp15-63

Harries, Elizabeth Wanning (2000) 'Donoghue, Emma' in *The Oxford Companion to Fairy Tales*. Jack Zipes (ed.) Oxford: Oxford University Press, pp134-35

Kavanagh, Linda. (1985) 'The Princesses' Forum' in *Rapunzel's Revenge: Fairytales for Feminists.* Anne Claffey, et al. (eds.) Dublin: Attic Press, pp5-11

Rowe, Karen E. (1999) 'To Spin a Yarn: The Female Voice in Folklore and Fairy Tale' in *The Classic Fairy Tales*, Maria Tatar (ed.) New York: Norton, pp297-308

Sipe, Lawrence R. (2000) "Those two gingerbread boys could be brothers': How Children Use Intertextual Connections During Storybook Readalouds' in *Children's Literature in Education,* 31, 2, pp73-90

Storr, Catherine (1995) *Clever Polly and the Stupid Wolf.* London: Puffin Books

Warner, Marina (1994) *From the Beast to the Blonde: On Fairy Tales and their Tellers.* London: Vintage

All There in Black and White: Examining Race and Ethnicity in Children's Literature

Karen Sands-O'Connor

> The stories in this book deal with race types.
> (Chance, 1901: 8)

Race and ethnicity have played an important role in children's literature. From the negative stereotypes found in nursery rhymes such as 'Taffy was a Welshman' and 'Ten Little Nigger Boys' to contemporary books for children that deal with racial and ethnic conflict, readers have been presented with a variety of ways of viewing difference, and critical scholarship in the field of children's literature has focused primarily on the effects these visions of difference have had on child readers. The reasons that authors write and children read about race and ethnicity are diverse but important, particularly since, as Peter Hunt argues, '[c]hildren's writers ... are in a position of singular responsibility in transmitting cultural values' (1994: 3). Race and ethnicity are critical elements of cultural production, but children's literature scholars' emphases on the child reader and the author's racial or ethnic affiliation have limited the possibilities for understanding the values cultures espouse. In order to expand our understanding of the importance of race and ethnicity, we must take a broader view of the literature written for children in this area.

The Child and the other: how and why we talk about race and ethnicity

> Little Indian, Sioux or Crow,
> Little frosty Eskimo,
> Little Turk or Japanee,
> O! don't you wish that you were me?
> (Stevenson, 1929: 36)

Any discussion of race and ethnicity in literature – for children or adults – is important in terms of highlighting societal and cultural attitudes at a given point in time. However, literature written for children is often assigned a higher level of concern, due to the assumed impressionable nature of its readers. Violet Harris, for example, insists that, 'the literacy achievement of African-American children would improve if they could see themselves and their experiences, history and culture reflected in the books they read' (1993: xvi). And Mawuena Kossi Logan comments that efforts to, 'trivialize the white supremacist myths in these old classics – namely those of Henty, Ballantyne, Marryat, Kingston – ... mistakenly claim that the imperialist perspectives came and went with an earlier era' (2001: 392). He adds dryly, '[s]uch biased attitudes supposedly make no impact on today's reader' (p392). Both Harris and Logan stress one of the major purposes critics discuss in literature about race and ethnicity: reader identification.

Both of these critics presume a fairly simplistic one-to-one correspondence between a reader and his or her racially- or ethnically-matched counterpart. In other words, if Black children see themselves represented positively in books, they will read and learn more. If White children see White characters as culturally superior, they will grow up with racist attitudes. While studies have borne out these notions to a certain extent (Elaine M. Aoki, in 'Turning the Page: Asian Pacific American Children's Literature' (1993) cites several of these studies), it is important to remember that reader-identification is not always so straightforward. John Stephens, in *Language and Ideology in Children's Fiction*, points out that, '[j]ust as the subject is constituted in sociality as a particular configuration of positions, so readers may be constituted by a range of available positions, and may select from a number of subject positions' (1992: 80). Thus, a female reader may well identify with a male protagonist, a Black reader's self-esteem may be strengthened by reading about a White character with whom he or she shares other similarities, and a White reader who identifies with a racist character may yet grow up espousing true racial harmony.

In addition, the whole concept of race as an either/or proposition is becoming increasingly blurred. Whereas historically, children who resulted from the union of two people of different racial backgrounds were considered to be **both** the product of a dominating, patriarchal, and racist society **and** a member, ultimately, of only one (usually the non-dominant) racial group, children in a similar situation today are beginning to be viewed differently. More contemporary multiracial unions originate as the result of deliberate and mutual choice by both parties than in the past, where such unions were often involuntary on the part of the non-dominant partner. And, as Francis Wardle suggests, a 'growing group of parents is insisting that the child has the ethnic, racial, cultural and genetic heritage of both parents' (1989: 10). For children with parents of two (or more) racial or ethnic groups, the assumption of identification with only one of those group's concerns, history, or culture is problematic.

While I am not arguing that identification is insignificant in a reader's perception both of books and of the surrounding world, I am suggesting that focusing on reader identification as the sole reason for publishing and promoting books about race and ethnicity is an increasingly untenable practice. As the plurality of the world increases, the likelihood that a simple connection can be made between the reader and any given character based on one aspect of a person's humanity steadily decreases.

Finally, the notion of reader identification is more complex in children's literature than in adult literature due to the socialising nature of children's literature. Pat Pinsent notes in *Children's Literature and the Politics of Equality* that 'children's authors in particular have frequently sought to teach their readers the values which society wants to encourage, even to the extent of seeking to indoctrinate them' (1997: 5). This statement of course presumes that the authors are fully aware of these encouraged values, and this can never entirely be the case. It also ignores the complicity of children's book authors with adult society; children need to be 'civilised' because they are not adults, just as 'savages' in the nineteenth century needed to be civilised because they were not White. Children's literature critics tend to disparage the latter but praise the former. In any children's book, therefore, child readers are forced into the position of split subject, torn between civilization (in the form of the adult world) and savagery (in the form of childhood). A child reader who is not only expected to civilise/socialise his or her way out of childhood but out of his or her notions about race and ethnicity faces an even greater challenge in terms of identification.

Children's literature critics have tended to view the portrayal of race and ethnicity as a process of identification and socialisation for the child reader, and because of this, the focus of study has been the reader and not the literature itself. While this focus is not without merit, it becomes increasingly problematic to determine what is beneficial or harmful to any given reader. It also relies on the validation of adult society to the detriment of child society and, ultimately, the validation of White society over non-White society. To examine literature that deals with the portrayal of race and ethnicity critically, it is important for the new generation of scholars to break out of rigid binary oppositions (White/Black, adult/child) and begin instead to focus on plurality, both in literature's content and meaning.

African-American children's literature: an international literature?

> Well, Daddy is going to own that building, 'cause I'm gonna fly over it and give it to him. Then it won't matter that he's not in their old union, or whether he's colored or a half-breed Indian, like they say.
> (Ringgold, 1991: np)

Children's literature scholars who want to focus on race or ethnicity have almost exclusively based their research on a single type of children's literature – African-American children's literature. Most of the scholarly books on race and ethnicity in children's literature, even when they do not concentrate solely on African-American literature, begin and end their discussion with it. Pat Pinsent's *Children's Literature and the Politics of Equality*, written by a British scholar and published by a British press, begins its chapter on 'Race and Ethnic Identity' with the idea that books such as Alice Walker's *The Color Purple* prove that 'the writers of such books are people who for one reason or another have been politicised by their own group's experience of prejudice, and have come to realise that equality issues can seldom, if ever, be viewed in isolation from each other' (1997: 91). Dianne Johnson concurs with this notion, writing that:

> African-American children's literature is an international literature not solely by force of definition, but because of the conscious and deliberate visions of a succession of writers and artists who from the emerging stages of this canon saw the world as a small place. Most importantly, they saw the world as a place in which words and images together can help people to be honest about who they are in both a personal and social/political, and thus, international context. (1995: 145)

African-American children's literature, according to these and many other critics, is a model for all literature concerned with racial and ethnic differences.

However, using African-American children's literature and its scholarship as the standard for any discussion of race and ethnicity raises many concerns. First, it places a preference on one group's issues, culture, and history over all others, thus continuing the cycle of dominance and oppression that many critics believe they are trying to redress. This is especially important in terms of the focus by African-American literary critics and authors on the oppression of their population within the United States. Due to the history of Africans and African-Americans in the US, this focus is understandable and useful for that particular literature – but this historical experience does not match that of other non-dominant groups around the world. The Scottish Highlanders in the 1700s certainly shared with African-Americans a sense of oppression – in their case, English law dictated everything down to the clothes they wore – but children's literature about the Highlanders (such as Robert Louis Stevenson's *Kidnapped*) suggests defiance of injustice as a more common theme than the oppression itself. If scholars were to take this literature as a model for discussion of race and ethnicity, this would alter both the criticism and scholarship. West Indians in the 1950s and 1960s had, in coming to Britain, more choice than did Africans coming to the United States in the 1700s and 1800s. This is not to say that the Black British population has not suffered oppression and racism from the predominantly White population – they certainly have – but the focus in a large percentage of the British children's literature about West Indians concerns the choice to assimilate or maintain traditions from the originating country. Again, using this focus as a way to discuss race and ethnicity would change the critical scholarship. These two examples are not meant to be all encompassing, but to suggest that considering African-American literature as an international literature in the sense that it can and should serve as a model and example for all struggles involving race and ethnicity, in fact only serves to provincialise the scholarship in this area.

African-American children's literature scholarship also puts a high value on a specific type of cultural authenticity that is not necessarily representative of views throughout the world. 'What counts,' says Nina Mikkelsen, 'is being an author with experiential understanding, usually gained through heritage (growing up in a particular ethnicity)' (1998: 37). Jacque Roethler adds, 'Black illustrators are more likely [than White illustrators] to understand the culture' (1998: 98). These sorts of critical attitudes have led to the extensive controversy over the place of books such as Mark Twain's *The Adventures of Huckleberry Finn* in the (children's) literary canon, but has also raised suggestions about even clearly well-intentioned authors and illustrators. Mary Thompson Williams and Helen Bush Caver, for example, fault the White author of *The Snowy Day*, Ezra Jack Keats, for letting 'his own background knowledge of stereotypes sometimes come through in his illustrations, such as size and clothing of female African-Americans' (1995: 19). Whether intentional or not, this focus on the inaccuracies of White authors and illustrators has led to an exclusionary scholarship that suggests no (or only the very rare) member of the dominant culture can accurately portray a non-dominant culture. Marc Aronson argues that this sets up a 'balkanization' of non-dominant literature that serves no one: '[t]he focus should not be on the identity of the creator, but rather on learning how to judge all manner of works on their own terms' (2001: 273). This does not mean ignoring race and ethnicity. It means focusing on their presentation within the novel.

In fact, many world societies have a broader view of who is capable of producing authentic depictions of non-dominant cultures. Beverley Naidoo and Niki Daly have both won awards for their depiction of Black South African communities, even though both are White. British author Mary Hoffman, also White, has won international acclaim for her series about a young Black British girl named Grace. Both Naidoo and Hoffman have racially-mixed families, so they are not without claim to cultural authenticity. However, neither author makes her own race or that of her family an issue in their choice of subject matter. Hoffman even goes so far as to suggest that 'Grace is really me – a little girl who loved stories' (np). For all these authors, writing and depicting race is simply the way they tell their stories.

Additionally, culturally authentic skin colour or ethnic background does not guarantee that the author/illustrator will avoid certain pitfalls of 'race books'. The much-applauded *Noughts and Crosses*, by Black British writer Malorie Blackman, relies on the eroticisation of the racial divide in order to explain why a militant White youth and the daughter of a powerful Black politician become lovers. Popular US author Walter Dean Myers has books containing sometimes stereotypical images of urban African-Americans, families headed by single mothers with teenage boys in gangs or in prison. For example, Faith Ringgold describes *Scorpions* perfectly when she comments that African-American artists:

> don't see themselves in this limited framework as always being a black family that is centered on a specific kind of adversity or pressure which is like a formula—the strong black mother and the father who's not there and the kid who's bad and can't read. It's not that way all the time. It's like that sometimes, but it would be nice to be able to have the different levels and shades of being that white men allow themselves to have. (1991: 12)

Ironically, Ringgold herself has been criticised for depicting stereotypes in *Tar Beach* because of the family's food choices of watermelon and fried chicken.

African-American children's literature and its critical scholarship have provided useful models for other non-dominant cultures attempting quality representation within books for children. But it is important to remember that African-American children's literature is just one type of literature, and cannot provide the only paradigm for understanding race and ethnicity in literature. Looking at other cultures and their histories will help provide new ways of understanding and discussing how and why we present race and ethnicity to children.

All there in black and white - but what (or who) are we looking for?

> Since then all the elephants have lived in peace. But recently the little ears and the big ears have been giving each other strange looks (McKee, 1990: np.)

Reader identification and cultural authenticity have been two major ways of considering children's literature that deals with non-dominant cultures, but they are both increasingly unhelpful as the categories of race and ethnicity become less clearly constituted. This is not to argue that the racial and ethnic aspects of children's literature are non-issues; I agree with Joel Taxel that it is impossible for 'authors of children's books, whether past or present, [to] operate in a political and ideological vacuum and pursue their artistic vision without constraint or limitation' (1997: 437). Therefore, as I research these issues in children's literature, I try to focus instead on *multiplicity* and *cultural construction.*

Difference will always be a topic in literature because difference causes conflict, whether racial, ethnic, religious, gender, or any other sort of difference. However, as various groups throughout the world intermarry and have children, those differences are becoming less easily identifiable. Thus, a scholarly discussion about race and ethnicity needs to start from a viewpoint of multiplicity. The questions must not be 'What race/ethnicity does this character or author belong to?' and 'Can a reader find racially/ethnically similar characters to identify with?' but instead, 'How does the author produce or display *multiple* definitions of race and ethnicity?' and 'Can any given reader identify with this character's humanity?' In this way, children's literature scholarship will begin to recognise that race and ethnicity are both ideas, created over time and by humans. Judith Butler, in *Gender Trouble*, calls categories such as race, gender, and ethnicity 'the political and cultural intersections' (1990: 3) that create identity. She goes on to say that these identities are 'tenuously constituted in time, instituted in an exterior space through a *stylized repetition of acts*' (p140). By examining the different ways that human categories are constituted, scholarly criticism will emphasise multiple ways of being a member of a racial or an ethnic group, and thus avoid the binary oppositions that lead to cultural domination by some groups over others.

In addition, a focus on cultural construction of race and ethnicity will allow scholars to envision the larger picture. Instead of examining a single racial or ethnic group, we will begin to see how race operates within the community that the book has created and that has created the book. Race and ethnicity do matter, but not in isolation. Connections between cultures, rather than differences, will be central, allowing *all* readers to become part of the conversation about this type of children's literature. The construction of race, as a trope, a character, or a literary device, will be one way – but not the only way – to understand children's literature with characters from non-dominant cultures. Thus, this literature will be able to avoid the isolation and ghettoisation it has faced in the past. Books will not be 'good African-American literature' but simply 'good literature' that anyone might enjoy. While this has long been a goal of many children's literature critics, the limited focus in scholarship has kept literature about race and ethnicity in a separate category, valued or decried because of its racial or ethnic quality only.

Children's literature uses various devices and enticements to entertain and socialise children to the world around them. Some authors and scholars have, up until now, used the device of difference in the form of race and ethnicity in order to tell a simplified version of the truth to children and the people that select books for children. This approach cannot succeed in the twenty-first century. Complex and serious ideas such as race and ethnicity deserve a complex and serious understanding. Only when we change our way of discussing race and ethnicity in children's literature will we finally **all** be there, in black and white.

Bibliography

Aoki, Elaine M. (1993) 'Turning the Page: Asian Pacific American children's literature' in *Teaching Multicultural Literature in Grades K-8,* Violet J. Harris (ed.). Norwood, Massachusetts: Christopher-Gordon, pp109-136

Aronson, Marc (2001) 'Slippery Slopes and Proliferating Prizes' in *Horn Book*, May-June, pp271-278

Butler, Judith (1990) *Gender Trouble.* London: Routledge.

Chance, Lulu Maude (1901) *Little Folks of Many Lands.* Boston: Atheneum

Graulich, Melody & Witzling, Mara (1994) 'The Freedom to Say What She Pleases: A Conversation With Faith Ringgold' in *NWSA Journal,* 6, 1, Spring, pp1-27

Harris, Violet J. (ed.) (1993) *Teaching Multicultural Literature in Grades K-8.* Norwood, Massachusetts: Christopher-Gordon

Hoffman, Mary. 'The Amazing Grace Story'
[Available at: http://www.maryhoffman.co.uk/grace.htm] (accessed 27/11/03)

Hunt, Peter (1994) *An Introduction to Children's Literature.* Oxford: Oxford University Press

Johnson, Dianne (1995) 'The International Context of African-American Children's Literature' in *The All-White World of Children's Books*, Osayimwense Osa (ed.) Trenton, New Jersey: Africa World Press, pp139-146

Logan, Mawuena Kossi (2001) 'Labour Party Reforms Versus Imperialist Literary Practice' in *The Lion and the Unicorn,* 25, 3, September, pp391-411

McKee, David (1990) *Tusk, Tusk.* London: Random House

Mikkelsen, Nina (1998) 'Insiders, Outsiders, and the Question of Authenticity: Who Shall Write for African-American Children?' in *African American Review,* 32, 1, Spring, pp33-49

Pinsent, Pat (1997) *Children's Literature and the Politics of Equality.* London: David Fulton

Ringgold, Faith (1991) *Tar Beach.* New York: Crown

Roethler, Jacque (1998) 'Reading in Color: Children's book illustration and identity Formation' in *African American Review,* 32, 1, Spring, pp95-105

Stephens, John (1992) *Language and Ideology in Children's Fiction.* London: Longman

Stevenson, Robert Louis (1929) *A Child's Garden of Verses.* New York: Platt and Munk

Taxel, Joel (1997) 'Multicultural Literature and the Politics of Reaction' in *Teachers College Record,* 98, 3, Spring, pp417-448

Wardle, Francis (1989) 'Children of Mixed Parentage: How' Can Professionals Respond?' in *Children Today* 18, 4, July-August, pp10-13

Williams, Mary Thompson & Caver Helen Bush (1995) 'African-Americans in Children's Literature – From Stereotype to Positive Representation' in *The All-White World of Children's Books*, Osayimwense Osa (ed.). Trenton, New Jersey: Africa World Press, pp13-32

A Publisher's Dilemma: The Place of the Child in the Publication of Children's Books

Laura Atkins

In this collection of essays which reflects on the relationship(s) between the child and adult as mediated through children's literature, one obvious relationship comes into play, but it is one that remains largely unexamined. Much has been written about the complex dynamic between the adult author and the child audience for whom that author writes. Jacqueline Rose reflects on the impossibility of an adult writing for the child that is not simply an authorial/adult construct in *The Case of Peter Pan* (1984), and Peter Hollindale writes of the concept of 'childness' and the ways in which the adult author relates to the child for whom he/she writes in *Signs of Childness in Children's Books* (1997). But what of the mammoth industry made up of adults who work on the literal construction of children's books? In the publishing industry, adults are not simply the authors of texts aimed at child readers, rather they exist as an organised group who select, edit, design, package and promote children's books to the market.

While within the academic study of children's literature we pay great attention to the analysis of books, little attention has been paid to their production. Most critics analyse the text as the unmediated voice of the author. Joel Taxel has noted this disparity in his recent essay 'Children's Literature at the Turn of the Century: Toward a Political Economy of the Publishing Industry' in which he writes that '[w]hile obvious to those *within* the industry, the impact of the business side of children's literature has not been given the sustained and systematic scrutiny it deserves by children's literature scholars and the educational community in general' (2002: 146). While seminal works such as Peter Hollindale's 'Ideology and the Children's Book' and John Stephens's *Language and Ideology in Children's Fiction* (1992) recognise that ideology shapes any text produced, few critics directly examine the force of the publishing industry. Many factors drive the editorial changes made to a submitted text, resulting in the ultimate published package. In this paper, I hope to shed some light on this process in order to reveal further the ideology that drives the production of children's literature, and which defines the child audience for whom the books are ostensibly produced. This essay will address the question: What are some of the forces which drive the development of children's books in today's publishing industry, and what role does consideration of the child reader play?

This essay comes through a combined personal and academic lens. Children's publishing is an industry with which I have been intimately involved, having worked within it for seven years. I came to the academic world of children's literature with an intense interest in the publishing process and how it shapes those texts that we study. In particular, I am interested in the editorial development of a manuscript – why a manuscript is acquired or rejected, and how and why it is changed once it has been acquired. In order to look more closely at the forces that come into play in the publishing of children's books, I will describe in detail the editorial acquisition and development of two books on which I was the editor. These examples will offer an opportunity to look at why a manuscript was acquired and what drove the editorial changes, as well as the degree to which consideration of the child reader affected the development of each book.

Sammy and the Dinosaurs (called *Harry and the Bucketful of Dinosaurs* in the original UK edition) was an import from England on which I worked as an assistant editor at Orchard Books in New York. In this picture book, a boy finds a bucket of toy dinosaurs that he cleans and takes everywhere. The dinosaurs whisper to him, and he looks-up their names at the library. The book's crisis takes place when he leaves the dinosaurs behind on a train, but is able to collect them from the lost property man when he tells him the dinosaurs' names. There are several reasons why I supported this book for acquisition. The writing is simple, using short and basic sentence structures such as: 'Harry took the dinosaurs downstairs. He unbent the bent ones. He fixed all the broken ones' (Whybrow, 1999: 7-8). I thought the simplicity in writing would be readily understood by young readers who are still learning *how* to read and understand a story. I also liked the fact that the book was about the relationship between a boy and his toy dinosaurs who are alive to him. J. A. Appleyard writes of the development of a child's reading in his book *Becoming a Reader* (1991), and refers to the early childhood reader as 'player', noting the close connection between the child's play with toys, literature which mirrors this play, and the parallel to a child's own development and learning. I was responding to this vision of childhood and reading when I selected this book as one that I thought would appeal to a child reader.

The biggest modification we made to *Sammy and the Dinosaurs* was to change the name of the main character from 'Harry' (his name in the British edition) to 'Sammy'. My recollection is that this change was made due to the popularity of Harry the dog, from books such as *Harry the Dirty Dog*. (In 1999, when we were editing the book, the now more famous Harry Potter was not such a cultural phenomenon). This was a group editorial decision, driven primarily by the marketing department. The name change was made based on anticipated market requirements, that since the name Harry had already been effectively branded in the United States of America, the name needed to be changed in order to make the character, and hence the book, stand out as original. Dan Hade comments on the increasing role of marketing in his article 'Storyselling: Are Publishers Changing the Way Children Read?' that '[t]he corporate owners of children's book publishing really aren't in the business of publishing children's books anymore. ... The business of corporate owners is developing brands' (2002: 512). In today's world in which children are exposed to tie-ins – where books are frequently merchandised as toys, TV shows, and movies – creating a unique brand becomes a priority in children's publishing, as it was when we decided to change the name from Harry to Sammy. Children's books are distinctive in that they are primarily purchased by adults – parents, teachers and librarians – rather than by the children who will read them. This is especially true of picture books. In today's juvenile publishing industry, which has become dominated by the corporate ownership of large media conglomerates (Hade writes that eight corporations dominate the industry in the United States of America), sales pressure has increased dramatically. Thus, a publisher's concern with sales will be highly influenced by the perceived desires of the adult purchaser.

Editing an import primarily means 'Americanising', or changing British words to American English. In the case of *Sammy and the Dinosaurs*, it meant changing words such as 'Nan' to 'Gran', 'garden centre' to 'garden center', and 'Lost Property Man' to 'Lost and Found man'. The Americanisation of books is generally based on the assumption that children will be uncomfortable when faced with unfamiliar spellings, words or locations. American editor Melanie Kroupa ascribes the lack of interest in foreign-feeling books to the child reader when she says, 'if things are too foreign or too English, American kids won't stick with it' (quoted in Whitehead, 1997: 29). Whitehead continues: 'In practice this means striking a balance between the foreign and the familiar, and reshaping texts to appeal to an audience whose attention is believed to be hard to engage and easy to lose' (p29). According to this construction, the North-American child reader is by and large reluctant, and only wants to read about familiar experiences in recognisable language. By Americanising the language in the book, we ascribed to this view of what the child reader will support, and more importantly, what will sell. As Susan Stan writes in 'Going Global: World Literature for American Children' about these types of changes, '[e]ditors make them because books labeled as 'too British' do not sell well' (1999: 175). This issue has been a controversial topic amongst the adults who buy, sell, and study juvenile literature, with many feeling that the homogenisation of children's books is robbing young people of exposure to different cultures, places, and language – a role that books can uniquely fulfill. Stan writes that '[s]uch changes detract from the authenticity of the work and deny American readers the opportunity to expand their knowledge and vocabularies' (p175). There is also concern that the erasure of cultural specificity results in a generic and less interesting book. This debate, which directly affects editorial decisions, is based upon various adults' perceptions of what a child will want to read, and ultimately driven by a concern for sales on the part of the publisher.

The second example is the book *DeShawn Days*, which is a collection of poems that together depict the life of a ten-year-old boy growing up in the projects (an American term, similar to a housing estate in England). The book originated as a few poems, which were submitted by the author, Tony Medina. I found in the poems a fresh voice that depicted the experience in a way I hadn't seen before, and one that felt especially childlike. For instance, the poem 'I Love Rap' expresses a child's appreciation for rap (a type of music which many children like, but which is not reflected in many books aimed at them) using straightforward language that seemed to me to be authentic to a ten-year-old. The poem begins:

> I love rap
> not just 'cause of the beats
> that make you move your feet
> but the words
> 'cause they talk about reality
> 'cause they talk about me
> and my block (2001: 19)

I appreciated the humour, as well as the darkness, in the poems, which seemed to me to reflect the complexity of children's lives, which are not always easy or happy (especially when living in poverty). Generally the poems were written in a direct way, expressing the emotions and reactions of the character, DeShawn. This seemed realistic to me, true to my own memories and perceptions of how children often see the world. I also appreciated that the poems offered a picture of an experience that is not often shown in the children's books that get published. All of these reasons are based on my own construction of childhood, and what should be available for children to read. And for these reasons, I sent the author editorial encouragement, and he wrote and submitted many more poems than were needed.

The author and I worked together to select and arrange the poems to create a portrait of the boy's life through verse. The poems included descriptions of DeShawn's asthma, his fears about his neighbourhood, and his relationship with his grandmother who is his primary caretaker. The choices were driven by Medina and myself applying our personal opinions, which were in and of themselves based on our cultural and ideological perspectives: which poems we thought were the strongest, which poems worked together to create an overall picture of this boy's life, and in what order these poems would be best placed. The child reader was in both of our minds as we went through this process, in terms of themes and language that we thought would appeal to children (such as a funny poem about competition between children in the same family, or the poem about DeShawn's love of rap music). We looked for themes that were at once universal (a child who cannot fall asleep and goes to his grandmother's bed for comfort), but also specific to an urban, poor environment such as the one in which the book takes place (DeShawn's asthma, his description of the sights and sounds of his neighbourhood). Within this editorial process, our individual constructions of the child reader played a fundamental role in the decisions that we made. Medina, who himself grew up in the projects, was concerned that the book portray this experience in a complex way, true to the grittiness of urban poverty. A political activist, he was driven by an agenda of creating books for children who do not otherwise get to see their lives depicted in most books, and in what he saw to be an honest way. My political leanings were in the same direction, so we generally agreed on the editorial shape and content of the book: our constructions of childhood and what is appropriate for children to read were generally aligned.

The acquisition process for this book was tricky. Once the author and I had selected the poems we thought best, the publisher was concerned that it was too dark and gritty to succeed as a picture book, particularly in the library and educational markets. This was based on assumptions about what is considered appropriate in a picture book, a notion that I will attempt to unpack. Certain poems were cut, such as one in which DeShawn goes to the hospital to be treated for asthma, while other, more upbeat and positive poems were requested. In the case of a poem entitled 'What is Life Like in the 'Hood?', which describes the neighbourhood where DeShawn lives, the words: 'crack vials everywhere' (p8) were seen as problematic. The Publisher felt strongly that the mention of crack should not be included in a picture book, that this would cause teachers or librarians not to buy it. With initial resistance from the author, this was eventually changed to '[p]eople walking everywhere' (p8). The Publisher's concern affected the final selection of poems, and the balance of dark to humorous themes that were ultimately included. Once he felt that balance had been met, and that the book represented a more positive vision, the book was acquired.

The development of *DeShawn Days* involved a great deal of discussion between the parties involved – the author and editor, as well as others working within the publishing company – which resulted in many editorial changes. As I have described, Medina and I applied our judgments and constructions of what we saw as appropriate for the child reader. In addition to this, the publisher's larger concern with the market and how it would respond to the book played a major role in its editorial development. A question at the heart of this process was: What will people accept in a children's book, and what should the balance be between what Medina saw as honestly representing an experience as opposed to reflecting an experience that the adult buyer will find acceptable *for children*? In looking at picture books about controversial topics (and specifically a book about drug addiction called *The House that Crack Built*), Dianne Koehnecke writes about different schools' responses to the book:

> Maughan's research showed that people in suburban neighborhoods tend to find the book appropriate for junior or senior high school students, while those in urban settings think children as young as first grade need exposure to the story. (2001: 25)

This statement gets to the heart of the issues that drove editorial development for *DeShawn Days*. The author had grown up in a situation similar to that described in the book, and he lived in Harlem at the time of its editorial development. His belief was that children living in this environment needed to see their reality accurately represented in children's books, while children who did not come from this experience should not be overly-protected from the realities of this world. However, as Koehnecke writes, teachers in different environments have very different conceptions of what is appropriate for children and at what age. Teachers are one of the primary consumers for whom publishers such as Lee & Low are producing their books. The child's needs here are constructed according to the perception of what the majority of teachers and librarians will accept, as perceived by the publisher whose concern is selling to that market. This fits into a model in which adults see children as innocents who should be protected. Rose writes about the origins of this approach: '[c]hildren's fiction has never completely severed its links with a philosophy which sets up the child as a pure point of origin in relation to language, sexuality and the state' (1984: 8). There is a schism between these points of view – those who want to represent the real world in what they perceive to be as honest a way as possible, and those who wish to protect the supposed innocence of the child for as long as possible. Both points of view are constructions of childhood, and the publishers find themselves in the middle of these differing positions.

The editorial development of *DeShawn Days* was based on a large array of adult conceptions of the child and childhood, as well as market concerns. This book exemplifies how political and complex the editorial process can be, based on who will buy the book, and on what is considered appropriate for children. In general, these reflections on the editorial development of two books bring up many questions, and expose several issues. A surprising revelation for those not intimately involved in the editorial process may be that the published text is often quite different from the author's original one, and the changes made are based on many factors. There is the consideration of perceived child-appeal, which especially affects the initial acquisition of a manuscript. In the case of a book imported from a 'foreign' culture, there is the adaptation to make the book as familiar and generic as possible. There are the constructions of childhood held by the author and editor in developing the manuscript. Finally, there is concern for the market that is based on the perceived desires of those who will buy the book. In addition to looking at the forces that drive editorial changes, I have also looked at the question of where the child fits in the publication process. I hope that I have shown some of the many conceptions of childhood which can drive the editorial development of texts; whether that is the idea that children are innocents to be protected, or beings who should be exposed to the realities of the world in a more complex and graphic way. These editorial examples have also shown that often the primary market considered in the editing and packaging of a book is not the child reader, but rather the teachers, librarians, and parents who will be buying the books.

Regardless of who the considered market is in the acquisition and editing of a book, even those texts developed with the child reader in mind are still based on adult conceptions of childhood. Hollindale writes of this issue: 'The author must construct childhood from an amalgam of personal retrospect, acquaintance with contemporary children, and an acquired system of beliefs as to what children are, and should be, like. Between the author and the child there is a cultural and historical gap ...' (1997: 12) This complicated nature of children's literature exists in the publishing world, which enacts the expectations of what children will want to read, and perhaps more importantly, what adults will want to *buy* for children. Stephens has a strong interest in the relationship between the author and audience in relation to children's literature. He writes:

> Writing for children is usually purposeful, its intention being to foster in the child reader a positive apperception of some socio-cultural values which, it is assumed, are shared by author and audience (1992: 3)

The process I have described has an important, even crucial role to play in Stephens's concept. The publisher becomes the embodiment of these assumed values shared by the author and the audience as it selects and produces the children's books that are available. But, in the case of the children's publishing industry, the concern with audience values is frequently the audience of adult purchasers of books for children. The publishers select the books deemed worthy of publication, and then shape those texts according to what they believe will sell to the purchasing adult. Even the perceptions held by editors and authors of what is appropriate for children varies, and these perceptions also drive the editing of children's books. The actual child, and the child's voice, are generally left out of the equation.

Bibliography

Appleyard, J. A. (1991) *Becoming a Reader: The Experience of Fiction from Childhood to Adulthood.* Cambridge: Cambridge University Press

Hade, Dan D. (2002) 'Storyselling: Are Publishers Changing the Way Children Read?' in *The Horn Book Magazine,* 78, 5, pp509-517

Hollindale, Peter (1988) 'Ideology and the Children's Book' in *Signal – Approaches to Children's Books 55.* Stroud: The Thimble Press, pp3-22

Hollindale, Peter (1997) *Signs of Childness in Children's Books.* Stroud: The Thimble Press

Koehnecke, Dianne (2001) '*Smoky Night* and *Crack*: Controversial Subjects in Current Children's Stories' in *Children's Literature in Education,* 32, 1, pp17-30

Medina, Tony (2001) *DeShawn Days.* Illus. R. Gregory Christie. New York: Lee & Low

Rose, Jacqueline (1984) *The Case of Peter Pan, or the Impossibility of Children's Fiction.* London: Macmillan

Stan, Susan (1999) 'Going Global: World Literature for American Children' in *Theory Into Practice,* 38, 3, pp168-178

Stephens, John (1992) *Language and Ideology in Children's Fiction.* London: Longman

Taxel, Joel (2002) 'Children's Literature at the Turn of the Century: Toward a Political Economy of the Publishing Industry' in *Research in the Teaching of English,* 37, 2, pp145-197

Whitehead, Jane (1997) ''This Is Not What I Wrote!': The Americanization of British Children's Books – Part II' in *The Horn Book Magazine,* 73, 1, pp27-34

Whybrow, Ian (1999a) *Harry and the Bucketful of Dinosaurs.* Illus. Adrian Reynolds. London: David and Charles Children's Books

Whybrow, Ian (1999b) *Sammy and the Dinosaurs.* New York: Orchard

Zion, Gene (1956) *Harry the Dirty Dog.* Illus. Margaret Bloy Graham. New York: HarperCollins

There's No Place Like Home: The Ideological and Mythological Construction of House and Home in Children's Literature

Ann Alston

How different is the portrait of the idealised home from the portrait of Peter Pan? Neither are affected by time and thus neither grow away from the ideal, perhaps as Rose suggests it is because 'someone prefers that [they] shouldn't' (1984: 3). The home is presented as a haven of family and idealised domesticity; it is an adult construct, an image that is so prominent that it has become naturalised. While sociologists and politicians often chart the demise of the family, the signs in children's books constantly reaffirm the position and importance of the family home: the dresser still appears, ordered and homely; the table comes complete with clean cloth; the houses often have four windows and a central door. The ideal home, like the ideal child, or indeed the ideal family is trapped in a past ideology, and adult writers, publishers, illustrators and readers seem to have little intention of letting the ideal of a 'good' family home grow into a fifteen storey tower block and indeed, if it were so, then it is highly probable that in it there would be a dresser, or cloth on the table, a symbol of domesticity and thus harmony.

A mythology of the perfect sanctuary of the home was developed to new levels in the nineteenth century; the Industrial Revolution led to an increasing number of the population working outside of the home and thus the home often became regarded as a haven from the outside world. Countless journals regarding the home became common, for example, the *Gardener's Magazine* was founded in 1826 (Tosh, 1999: 33); the first citation of the word 'homesick' appeared in the *OED* and phrases like 'Home Sweet Home' expressed the Victorians' 'deep commitment to the *idea* of home' (p27). It is interesting then that this concept of the home as a perfect retreat is maintained in all aspects of culture, but predominantly children's fiction, to this very day. Through children's books the child reader is instantly immersed in a cultural ideology; one that is comfortable and familiar where everyone knows his/her place. For what must be accounted for here is that this is an adult's presentation of culture; thus, in short, to study children's literature is to analyse an adult ideal (Hunt, 1994: 3). It comes as no surprise then that houses in children's literature are often overflowing with signs of domesticity and thus before analysing the wider implications of this it is worth looking at a few examples of the perfect homes that have been presented in children's books, firstly, by focusing on the idealistic homes that exist over a century long time span and secondly, by looking at the homes that appear to fall short of the traditional ideal.

To begin with the idealistic homes it is striking that even in animal-based texts small furry animals often have cosy, idealised homes: consider Mole or Badger in *The Wind and The Willows*, Mr Tumnus or the Badgers in *The Lion, The Witch and the Wardrobe* or more recently, the mice in *Angelina Ballerina*. The dressers, neat, tidy and ordered symbolise civilisation, adult order within the family, a nurturing home. The food on the table, or hams hung up, emphasise a well nourished family; the home is giving food and shelter and is therefore reinforcing the image of itself as a safe haven. The beams, just evident, signify a cosy, warm home that, like the March's home, 'is a nice place, though it isn't splendid' (Alcott, 2000: 134). Similarly, the illustrations from *Milly-Molly-Mandy* to Jill Murphy's *All in One Piece* to Jacqueline Wilson's texts show a host of domestic signs. The text in *Milly-Molly-Mandy* is preceded by a map of the village, in which there are thatched cottages all labelled as to who they belong to – a church, a school and corner shops – while inside the house the family are pictured eating their meal together round the table with a cloth with a dresser in the background, and the father at the head.

The image of the home and surrounding village seen in *Milly-Molly-Mandy* is not simply a product of the 1920s for in *All in One Piece* the children are pictured sitting round the table (somewhat messily, granted), eating their meal, again with the adult ordered dresser behind them and a child's picture, not uninterestingly, of an elephant outside his castle, on the wall. As the parents go out for the evening they turn to see another idealised, somewhat clichéd, image of the home as the children and Granny wave from the lighted window; home again is sanctuary. These clichés in children's fiction are powerful methods of enhancing control, as Beer points out 'cliché assures us that we all belong together' (1997: 29). In constantly reworking the clichés of domestic signs, the child reader is embedded in an adult culture of the home, is told that he/she belongs in a certain system, a system that reassures adults of the home as haven.

To move on to the second part of the analysis which focuses on the non idealistic home it is essential to turn to the criticism which emphasises the loss of home and family within contemporary children's fiction. Lucy Waddey argues that 'in more recent fiction, attitudes towards home and parents have changed; indeed one mark of contemporary realism for children is its ambivalent description of home and family life' (1983: 13). In some ways this is true but I think that it is fair to say that an ideal of home is always presented, and this ideal is firmly rooted in the images of cosy homes that are constantly emphasised in children's literature. The family house, enclosed from the rest of the world, has not lost its value because some texts do not have it, indeed, by describing those families that do not have it as somewhat inadequate, the value of the ideal house in children's literature is actually enhanced. The characters in Jacqueline Wilson's texts constantly yearn for 'a normal family' in *The Bed and Breakfast Star*, Elsa and her family go out for dinner and Elsa tells the reader that they 'looked like an ordinary, happy family having a meal out. But we didn't go back to an ordinary happy family house' (1995: 56). The house is an important sign in indicating the contentment of the family. In addition, in Jacqueline Wilson's *Double Act* the rebirth of the new family is shown to be successful by an illustration in which the family share a meal together (2000: 157). In many ways, it would be difficult to find a more idealistic illustration of the family; they sit round the table, the food is not only home-cooked, but cooked by the mother figure, there is a homely picture on the wall and a cloth on the table. The ideal of home and family are still adhered to, the together family, based on a myth that was heightened during the nineteenth century, remained the happy ending at the end of the twentieth century. Indeed, the illustration could be from any time period over the last century, if anything, it looked somewhat dated at the end of the twentieth century, but in children's books the image prevails as it constantly re-emphasises a static middle class perspective.

The 'good' family/home is in fact enhanced by the image of the non-conforming and thus 'bad' family home. Families that are not 'normal' can be recognised by the illustrations of their homes and the objects within the home. In Roald Dahl's *Matilda* any experience of the signs in children's literature will inform the reader that the Wormwoods are 'bad'; rather than sitting round the table to eat their evening meal, the family sit on the sofa and watch the television. In opposition to this, Miss Honey lives in a rural cottage that 'looked more like a doll's house than a human cottage' (1988: 184), and later when she moves into her rightful home after the demise of Miss Trunchbull, Matilda and Miss Honey are pictured sitting at the table having afternoon tea with a dresser in the background. The dresser has appeared and thus the reader is reassured that Miss Honey and Matilda will live happily ever after in domestic harmony. The images of home presented in children's fiction are powerful and political for they re-assert, re-emphasise and construct identities and ideals that are all based on a myth.

It is not surprising, given these images of home in children's literature, that as Virginia L. Wolf points out 'our desire for home, rooted in our infantile perception of reality, is so strong that we cannot do without the myth' (1990: 66). It seems to me, however, that this resembles something of a chicken and egg theory; the desire for home is rooted in adult psyche partly because of the illustrations and ideas that adults encountered as children in children's books. As a result, adults continue to produce texts showing ideals of home and thus children's literature remains trapped in a circular pattern, hence the century long time span of the given examples. (It must be added that there are some examples of children's fiction that are moving away from this, for example, Aidan Chambers's or Melvin Burgess's work, but these are the exceptions to what is quite a strong pattern of idealised homes and families). This perhaps gives a somewhat static feel to children's literature, but this preservation of certain ideals can be considered in opposing ways: static images are secure giving adults (and it must be remembered that most children become adults) a constant path back to childhood nostalgia, but these images can also be considered to be outdated, unrealistic and therefore unfair ways of presenting the world to children. An untrue world loaded with cultural clichés is being presented. Wolf goes on to write that though she celebrates the 'wonderful mythic houses in children's literature as an invaluable legacy of comfort' she worries that 'they deny too much of a reality' (1990: 66), the opposition between adult comfort and an awkward feeling of promoting a world that does not prepare the child for life is one that is frequently addressed and then it seems forgotten about; adults refuse to let go of nostalgic images and ideals.

To search for what is true and what is not, however, is something of an elusive task, for in the light of Barthes's analyses the images/clichés that are presented to society become naturalised, become the world:

> The whole of France is steeped in this anonymous ideology: our press, our films, our theatre, our pulp literature, our rituals, our Justice, our diplomacy, our conversations, our remarks about the weather, a murder trial, a touching wedding, the cooking we dream of, the garments we wear, everything, in everyday life, is dependent on the representation which the bourgeoisie *has and makes us have* of the relations between man and the world. These 'normalized' forms attract little attention, by the very fact of their extension, in which their origin is easily lost. (2000: 140)

The clichés of dressers, tablecloths and pictures on the walls in homes in children's books are part of this naturalised myth, are clichés that have become, by their constant reappearance, a reality, something to attain; for if, as an adult, the house with roses round the door, dressers and meals with the family round the table can be attained then the adult has been successful, has lived up to the image in the children's book. Of course, the perfect home is not an ideal reserved to the pages of children's literature, it is reworked in all parts of our culture, but in children's literature it seems more abundant, more exaggerated; children's literature in some ways is the playground of the adult dreamer, a place of adult self-indulgence. Children's literature, as has been commented upon many times, does not belong to children, but to adults, indeed it is something that adults use in order to take 'privileged positions in determining the value of a literature for young readers' (Zipes, 2002: 40).

Perhaps this placement of the privileged adult might not be considered entirely 'fair' on children, but it seems that there are few alternatives. Adults will always write, publish and buy the literature, and in the writing of children's literature adults will continue to retreat to the remembered images of their own childhood, and encourage children to enjoy the same images and ideals – in short, live similar lives. Indeed, new objects, especially those deemed unfashionable by adults, take some time to permeate their way into children's literature, take the illustration of the television for example, (although it obviously would not appear in *Wind in the Willows*, or *Milly-Molly-Mandy*) it does not appear in either *Angelina Ballerina* or *All in One Piece* despite the illustrations being centred on the lounge and kitchen, in addition, when the television appears in *Matilda* it is used as a sign of a 'bad' family. Quite apart from reality in which most families will have a television, in a constructed world of the home in children's fiction it is often ignored; the adult writer/illustrator prefers to ignore what is not deemed ideal, what may not have been so significant in his/her childhood.

The adult then only allows a secure reflection of the way he/she would like the world to be to appear in children's literature, this world is a familiar, culturally loaded one which places the adult in complete power as Nodelman makes clear:

> [w]hat we believe about how we must control or shelter our children defines their power in relation to ourselves as adults. And whatever else literary texts are, and whatever pleasure they might afford us, they are also expressions of the values and assumptions of a culture and a significant way of embedding readers in those values and assumptions. (1996: 68)

Indeed, so the spaces and symbols of domesticity in children's literature simply reassert adult prominence and adult ideals. This can be related to postcolonial discourse as in discussing space, landscape and home Radhika Mohanram suggests that 'place/landscape are saturated with relations of domination which are relevant to the construction of identity' (1999: xv). In children's literature the child's identity with regard to home is constructed by the images of the home that surround him, the child, if he/she is part of a 'normal' family, will be surrounded by the signs of domesticity. These symbols of domesticity are adult ones, surely few children want or are interested in dressers in the background be they of a text or a real home, and thus the child's own self identity is dominated by adult orientated images and signs. The child in all ways is dominated by the adult; familiarised into an adult world, one that adults can understand in the same way as the natives in colonial fiction are often described in terms that the colonialists understand, the child like those who are colonised, is always the weaker one of the two, and the book by immersing the child into an adult ideal is able to control the child.

When children draw pictures then, the four windows and a door appeal to an adult sense of home, they reflect the home that the adult has presented to the child in literature, it is an ideological concept. Politically, the house is a western house, and the texts above present illustrations of very British homes; the teapots, the roast dinners, the floral aprons, the dressers, the armchairs round the fire and countless other signs. The home is littered with domestic and also national symbols, it is familiar to the adult at all times. Indeed, even when children in texts like *The Famous Five* or *Swallows and Amazons* series stay away from home, as they camp, they reproduce a microcosm of home in which the siblings sit round a picnic rug to eat their traditional food. The unfamiliar, and this is the unfamiliar to the child character and to a certain extent the adult writer/reader, is domesticated and thus familiarised once again into an adult ideology.

In discussing the home, we are in essence, discussing the family for as John Tosh argues 'at a symbolic level the family became indistinguishable from the domestic space which it occupied' (1999: 4). The family is a constant source of anxiety and concern in society, but if in children's literature the ideals of the home do not change, then it follows that the ideal of the family also remains static. To keep producing these ideals/clichés is to enter a perpetual circle of unchanging children's literature, a literature that places expectations in children's minds of how they should grow up and live, essentially, of the home that they should be able to provide for their children. This home may well be a fiction, an unattainable dream. So then this poses the dilemma of whether children's fiction is shaped by the world around it, or plays a significant role in shaping the world. The answer is perhaps both: surely adult writers are affected by surrounding images (as has been noted it is not only children's literature that promotes an ideal of home/family), and yet the deep seated dreams and ideals of many may well have been initiated in the reading of a children's book, the first introduction into an adult ideology. Indeed the possible effect of a children's book on an individual is illustrated in Ann Thwaite's biography of Frances Hodgson Burnet in which she states that during her childhood, *The Secret Garden* 'became part of my own life' (1991: ix). To read a book with a toddler then is not just to pass five minutes but to introduce him/her to a society, to a system of signs, these signs are important for in their didacticism they do not simply offer a sense of nostalgia to the adult, but promote a certain way of life to the child. The adult with the opportunity may well build a home with a cottage feel, roses around the door and dressers in the background, or indeed, a child may have grown up surrounded by these objects, but certainly, not all the adults will be able to achieve this 'dream' home in the same way as not all the children will have grown up in such a home. Children's literature then constantly re-emphasises a myth, but this myth is entirely western, entirely middle class. The study of the book in children's literature is an important one, the myths and clichés presented offer valuable material for both a historicist and sociological perspective, but with regards to the position of the child in children's literature, the study is somewhat static, trapped in a circle of adult, middle class ideology.

Bibliography

Alcott, Louisa May (2000) *Little Women.* First published in 1868. Harmondsworth: Penguin Books

Barthes, Roland (2000) *Mythologies.* London: Vintage

Beer, Gillian (1997) 'The Making of a Cliché: No Man is an Island' in *Fonctions du Cliché du Banal à la Violence*, Claudine Raynaud & Peter Vernon (eds.). Tours: Presses Universitaires François Rabelais, pp29-41

Blyton, Enid (1997) *The Famous Five: Five on Treasure Island.* First published in 1942. London: Hodder Children's Books

Brisley, Joyce Lancaster (1949) *Milly-Molly-Mandy Stories.* First published in 1928. London: George Harrap

Dahl, Roald (1988) *Matilda.* Illus. Quentin Blake. London: Jonathon Cape

Grahame, Kenneth (1973) *The Wind in The Willows.* First published in 1908. Illus. E. H. Shepard. London: Methuen

Holabird, Katharine (1987) *Angelina Ballerina.* Illus. Helen Craig. First published in 1983. Harmondsworth: Penguin Books

Hunt, Peter (1994) *An Introduction to Children's Literature.* Oxford: Oxford University Press

Lewis, Clive Staples (2001) *The Lion, the Witch and the Wardrobe.* Illus. Pauline Baynes. First published in 1950. London: Collins

Mohanram, Radhika (1999) *Black Body: Women, Colonialism and Space.* Minneapolis: University of Minnesota Press

Murphy, Jill (1998) *The Large Family: All in One Piece.* First published in 1987. London: Walker Books

Nodelman, Perry (1996) *The Pleasures of Children's Literature.* New York: Longman Publishers USA

Ransome, Arthur (1993) *Swallows and Amazons.* First published in 1930. London: Red Fox

Rose, Jacqueline (1984) *The Case of Peter Pan, or the Impossibility of Children's Fiction.* London: Macmillan

Thwaite, Ann (1991) *Waiting for the Party: The Life of Frances Hodgson Burnett.* Boston: Nonpariel

Tosh, John (1999) *Masculinity and the Middle-class Home in Victorian England.* New Haven & London: Yale University Press.

Waddey, Lucy (1983) 'Home in Children's Fiction: Three Patterns' in *Children's Literature Association Quarterly*, 8, 1, pp13-15

Wilson, Jacqueline (1995) *The Bed and Breakfast Star.* Illus. Nick Sharrat. First published in 1994. London: Corgi Yearling Books

Wilson, Jacqueline (2002) *Double Act.* Illus. Nick Sharrat and Sue Heap. First published in 1995. London: Corgi Yearling Books

Wolf, Virginia L. (1990) 'From the Myth to the Wake of Home: Literary Houses' in *Children's Literature 18*, pp53-67

Zipes, Jack (2002) Sticks and Stones – The Troublesome Success of Children's Literature from Slovenly Peter to Harry Potter. London: Routledge

Border Crossings: *Carrie's War*, Children's Literature and Hybridity

David Rudd

In her groundbreaking work, *The Case of Peter Pan, or the Impossibility of Children's Fiction*, Jacqueline Rose propounds that children's fiction is impossible, not because it cannot be written, but because it is based on a contradiction, purporting to be about children, when it is really about adults, who figure the child for their own purposes, as a space where the anxieties of adulthood can be held at bay. Against the insecurities of sex, language, identity, and existence, the figure of the child stands as a bulwark: a secure point of origin that occludes doubt. While I agree with the main thrust of Rose's case, I would take issue with her that Peter Pan is exceptional in exhibiting this impossibility, in 'going too far' (Rose, 1984: 70). In other words, the notion that '[w]riters for children' should not disturb any 'psychic barriers ... the most important of which is the barrier between adult and child' (p70), rests on a disavowal that is regularly troubled, I would argue. It is precisely because of a knowledge of the fragility of their adult selves ('who they are') that writers for children seek to shore up the psychic barriers; but the 'faultlines', to use Alan Sinfield's helpful term (1992), are still there, to be read by either party.

The shift in emphasis that I am suggesting parallels the response that Homi Bhabha (1994) made to Edward Said's work on colonialism. In children's literature, Rose herself uses the notion of the child as a colonised being to capture the way that children's literature is imposed on the young reader, seeking to secure him or her. Perry Nodelman (1992) has also noted the parallels, showing how readily 'the child' can be substituted for 'the orient' in Said's *Orientalism* (1978). However, Bhabha gives Said's work a more psychoanalytical emphasis, suggesting that the relation between coloniser and colonised is less secure, in that the former is always troubled by the relation between the two (see Rudd (2004) for details).

I shall use Nina Bawden's *Carrie's War* (1973) to exemplify my case, not because it is special – as Rose sometimes seems to suggest of *Peter Pan* – but, rather, because it is more representative. This said, *Carrie's War* is certainly a rich text, as work by others has shown (e.g. Lissa Paul, 1998), and stages clearly the issues I want to consider. Bawden is also fascinating in that she herself has repeatedly expressed her interest in the tension between adults and children: '[s]ince it was the adults who had written these [children's] books', she recalls thinking when young, 'it was reasonable to assume that they didn't want to give themselves away; show themselves to us children, to their *enemies*, as they really were.' Adults she saw as 'uncertain, awkward, quirky, *dangerous* creatures', whom she wanted to '*expose*' (1974: 7). Of course, it might be argued, there is a certain duplicity here, given that Bawden herself writes from an adult perspective. But this is irrelevant to my point, which is concerned with the staging of cultural difference, something that Bawden's novel enacts.

Briefly, *Carrie's War* is the story of the eponymous Carrie and her younger brother, Nick, dispatched to Wales as evacuees during World War II, where they are reluctantly housed by Councillor Evans and his younger sister, Lou. Their lives become richer, though, when they meet Evans's older sister, Mrs Dilys Gotobed, her simple-minded adult relation, Johnny, and their housekeeper, Hepzibah Green, with whom another evacuee, the studious Albert Sandwich, is staying. The enmity between Councillor Evans and his older sister causes Carrie great distress – something that she 'carries' into adult life, and which is only resolved (partially) when she returns to Wales with her own children.

Though the war that Carrie experiences is obviously external, it is more significantly psychological, involving warring impulses that Carrie not only suffers as a child, but which continue to distress her. In the first chapter, we see the adult Carrie wrestling with these issues, eventually regressing before her own children's eyes, so that she has less the 'tone ... of a grown-up' (1973: 13), becoming 'more like a cross girl' (p18). Her 'talking cure' then commences, as she enters 'the zone of occult instability where the people dwell', to recycle Fanon's phrase (Bhabha, 1994: 35). And as Bawden depicts it, this repressed zone also offers resistance, akin to 'pushing through a forgotten forest in a fairy tale. The tangled wood round Sleeping Beauty's castle' (p10).

This realm is 'the point at which there is a loss of meaning in the contestation and articulation of everyday life, between classes, genders, races, nations' (Bhabha: 34). All these divisions are certainly contested, the last between Welsh- and Englishness, but so too is one other division: that between adult- and childhood. We enter an area where certainties are left behind, an area of hybridity, where 'the symmetry and duality of self/ other, inside/ outside' breaks down, where 'the settler-n-ative [sic] boundary' becomes 'anxious and ambivalent' (Bhabha: 116).

From the outset the children are unequivocally depicted as subalterns, arriving with 'their names on cards round their necks. Labelled like parcels ... only with no address to be sent to' (p20); then told to '[s]tand ... by the wall,' where 'someone will choose' them in a 'kind of cattle auction' (p23), as Albert describes it. Parallels with slavery are also evident:

> Someone had stopped in front of her [Carrie]. Someone said, "Surely you can take two, Miss Evans?"
> "Two girls, perhaps. Not a boy and a girl, I'm afraid." (p24)

Carrie is the vortex round which these warring tendencies whirl, she herself experiencing a sense of inauthenticity. As her name suggests, Carrie is forever a go-between, mouthing, or mimicking, the voices of others. She is a hybrid being, neither adult nor child but an '*in-between* space', which 'carries the burden of the meaning of culture' (Bhabha: 38); this is also, potentially, a traumatic space: 'I feel *torn* in two' (Bawden, 1973: 130), as she complains at one point. And focalised through Carrie's interstitial consciousness, the novel interrogates each of these terms, adult and child, showing that neither is authentic, neither is securely grounded.

Because of the dynamic, unsettled nature of his project, Bhabha deploys various terms to express the colonial relationship – 'ambivalence', 'stereotype', 'mimicry' and 'hybridity' – each containing its own 'ambivalence' in the psychoanalytic sense of experiencing conflicting tendencies. In Carrie's case, her sense of selfhood, normally confirmed by her mother, has been removed, and she finds her identity in doubt. Her being has no core; emptily she 'carries' the words and actions of others, speaking 'in a grown-up voice like her mother's' (p21), then imitating new voices around her, like Mr Evans's: 'She said, "Then want must be your master, Nicholas Peter Willow"' (p64). Mimicking them, however, does nothing to help her discover a voice of her own; in fact, it leads her to question the authenticity of others'.

Mr Evans is presented as a self-important coloniser, his name in capitals over his shop front. His sister, Lou, informs the two children that 'he's a Councillor ... a very important man' (p27). His authority derives from a number of institutional sites, whose discourses he espouses. Certainly he is a patriarchal figure, who bullies not only his sister, to whom he's 'more like a father ... than a brother' (p34), but also 'the women who came into his shop' (p31); in fact, he's annoyed that his evacuees are not exclusively female: 'I told her, you fetch two girls now' (p32). Because of his importance, Auntie Lou (as she asks the children to call her), advises them to address him as 'Mr Evans.' His patriarchal power is endorsed not only by his status as councillor, but also by his religion, he being 'very strong Chapel' (p26). In the children's room is a framed notice in black, stating 'The Eye Of The Lord Is Upon You' (p26), punning on Evans's status as an all-seeing eye/I, itself reinforced by the intimidating 'pictures of dead, bearded Chapel Elders looking down from the walls' (p38) of the local chapels. However, as Bhabha says, although 'the authorities ... keep an eye on them [the colonised], their proliferating difference evades that eye, escapes that surveillance' (1994: 112). Here, there is a distinct evasion, in that the chapels are being used as schools with English, non-chapel teachers, thus separating out education and religion, such that Carrie finds school '[m]ore *fun*' (p38) in Wales.

From the children's arrival, then, Mr Evans finds his authority under threat, despite his attempts to make the children like Naipaul's 'mimic men'

(Bhabha, 1994: 88) giving them Bibles for presents, having them help in his shop, and even seeking to enlist Carrie in his surveillance work, to spy on the Gotobed household, 'it might be a good idea to get her to go there sometimes, keep her eyes open' (p67).

Theorising this sense of anxiety and the slippage caused in the process of trying to produce like-minded beings, Bhabha draws on Lacan's notion of the mirror stage, where a subject, seeing their own image, experiences an exhilarating sense of wholeness, which the other reflects. In Evans's case, this narcissistic feeling is furnished by his sister Lou, with the community playing its own supporting role. However, as Lacan makes plain, this wholeness is an illusion: it is but an image, an 'Imaginary' wholeness. Aside from narcissism, then, 'aggressivity' is also produced, in that the image is '*the same but not quite*' (Bhabha 89) and is, therefore, 'potentially confrontational' (p77). The colonised other (such as the child), can accentuate this difference, being only a '*metonymy of presence*' (p89). Like a fetish, the child is reassuringly similar to the adult, providing an image of uncastrated completeness, a figure of 'pure origin' (p75). But simultaneously, the child's presence masks difference: it is *not* an adult; it behaves differently – which, of course, threatens the adult's wholesome identity. In this way, 'the look of surveillance returns as the displacing gaze of the disciplined, where the observer becomes the observed and 'partial' representation rearticulates the whole notion of *identity* and alienates it from essence' (p89).

Nick is particularly effective in showing 'the 'signs' or 'marks' of authority' as nothing 'more than 'empty' presences of strategic devices' (p113). Evans thus finds his own authoritative discourses developing an unfortunately ironic tone, as, for instance, when he lays down the rules of the house:

> "... no shouting, or running upstairs, and no Language." Nick looked at him and he went on – quickly, as If he knew what was coming, "No *Bad* Language, that is." (Bawden, 1973: 33)

When Evans raises the issue of bed wetting, Nick retorts, "[t]hat's a rude thing to mention," effectively upbraiding the adult for using inappropriate 'Language.' Evans, we are informed, 'looked startled – as if a worm had just lifted its head and answered him back' (p32). When Evans leaves the room, Nick capitalises on his victory in front of Auntie Lou: "[y]ou don't mind Language, do you? I mean, I don't know the deaf and dumb alphabet" (p33). Evans does not intimidate Nick because Nick has noticed that this authoritative voice comes from between 'false teeth that clicked when he talked.' As Nick says, "[y]ou can't really be scared of someone whose teeth might fall out" (p32). So, when Nick upbraids Evans for his rudeness, it is of note that 'Nick's gaze was fixed on Mr Evans's mouth' (p32). This makes Aunt Lou's remark that her brother's 'bark's worse than his bite' (p33) more ironic. Evans's false teeth, fetish-like, cover (and uncover) his symbolic castration; that is, his awareness of his own flawed identity.

As Bhabha says, '[i]t is not that the voice of authority is at a loss for words. It is, rather, that the colonial discourse has reached that point when, faced with the hybridity of its objects, the *presence* of power is revealed as something other than what its rules of recognition assert' (1994: 112). With the help of Nick and Carrie, the browbeaten, childlike Auntie Lou also starts to resist, as demonstrated by her response to Evans's protests over her singing: 'We're supposed to make a joyful noise unto the lord, aren't we, Samuel?' (Bawden, 1973: 99) Evans finds his words returning from a new social location, disrupting their authenticity and querying his own presence. Not only is she using the empowering discourse of 'the lord', familiar to Evans, but she is also empowered in self-image, aided – unbeknownst to Evans – by her American boyfriend. Evans's subsequent awareness that she has chosen the American over him cements his downfall. Previously, brother and sister had a typical master-slave relationship, captured in Carrie's description of Lou's 'thin squeak' of a voice in contrast to Evans's 'roar.' It's '[l]ike a mouse answering a lion' (p30), as she puts it. But, just like the lion in Aesop's fable, Evans learns how dependent he has been on Lou's narcissistic presence. Significantly, the morning after her departure, Carrie mistakes Evans's scratching noise for 'rats', then discovers him complaining that he has been made to 'look small' (p147). He is not quite 'at a loss for words', but he has lost the self-assured rhetoric of the adult coloniser. He sits at 'the dead fire' (p145) of their hearth, realising that the worm has indeed turned, that Heim has turned unheimlich. Soon after this, we are later informed, Evans dies.

Being closest to the colonising discourses of power, Evans is most susceptible to their disruption. But there is a doubling here, and further slippage. For Evans is himself a mimic man, displaced by earlier colonisers. In Bhabha's terms, Evans is not so much 'confronted by' as 'tethered to ... his dark reflection, the shadow of colonized man, that ... breaches his boundaries, repeats his action at a distance, disturbs and divides the very time of his being' (1994: 44). Evans is from a Welsh, working-class background, originally working as a miner, the job that killed his father. The colonial dimension is foregrounded because Evans's older sister, Dilys Gotobed, married not just an Englishman, but a capitalist, mine-owning one. The doubling is made more explicit when Evans shows Carrie a picture of his sister and him, commenting, 'I'd be ten years, about. Dilys a bit older' (Bawden: 147) – the same age as Nick and Carrie, in fact. There are other parallels, too. Nick, for instance, accuses Carrie of going over to the enemy – that is, to the coloniser, Mr Evans – which is just what Evans accused his sister of doing.

Druid's Bottom, where the Gotobeds live, functions as Evans's unconscious, the name itself conjuring up notions of primitive, repressed material – the antithesis of both his 'Chapel' and its 'Language.' The Gotobeds' colonising background is made explicit, too. 'They made their money out of sugar and slaves' (p59), we learn. There is a skull, reputedly of a slave boy, still in the house which, for superstitious reasons, is not to be removed, for fear of something bad ensuing. Its uncanny presence becomes particularly significant for Carrie, who eventually hurls it into a nearby pond, thereby holding herself responsible for a fire that all but destroys the house (there are echoes of *Jane Eyre* here, too).

What Bhabha refers to as the subject's fantasy of occupying 'the master's place while keeping his [subaltern] place in the slave's *avenging* anger' (p44) is played out for the reader in the course of the book, partly through Carrie's action, but also through Albert's (as we learn towards the end). Albert repeatedly refuses to classify people by age: 'I don't see what difference it makes, people's ages', he says, treating Nick as if he 'was a boy the same age', and also making friends of Hepzibah and the '*ancient*' Mrs Gotobed (pp76-7). Age is still an impediment for Albert, though, when it comes to establishing Hepzibah and Johnny's right to go on living in Mrs Gotobed's house after her death. Despite his rational interpretation of events he cannot implement anything because he is a child, lacking adult rights and status. He imagines what would happen if he took the issue to a solicitor:

> I could just hear Mr Rhys saying, *Run away, little man, back to your comics!* ... I wish I was grown-up ... It's a fearful *handicap* being a child. You have to stand there and watch, you can never make anything happen. ... If I was grown-up, I could stop *this.* (pp128-30)

Children are indeed '*almost the same but not quite*' (Bhabha, 1994: 89). But if adulthood can be so effectively imitated, as Albert shows, it raises the question of what is so special about it in the first place, particularly when we look at the far-more childish behaviour of some of the grown-up characters. Evans and his older sister, Dilys, are prime examples, but there are others, like Evans's adult son, Frederick, who is shown to be a greedy bully, especially in the scene where he taunts Johnny Gotobed. The latter, of course, is an adult in body and strength, but a child in mind. It is certainly ironic that Albert has to wait until he is an adult before he can finally do something to help Johnny and Hepzibah.

Parallels with the World War, evident elsewhere, are particularly noticeable here in the marginal status of these two migrant figures: the 'witch' (as she is known), and the simpleton. Both of these celebrated types have been persecuted in European history, the latter falling within the remit of Hitler's 'final solution'. Frederick's bullying tactics, taunting and assaulting Johnny, arguing that a 'vicious loony like that' should be 'locked up' (Bawden: 104), are obviously meant to bring these parallels to mind. Which brings us back to Bhabha and the dangers of essentialist notions of gender, race and nationhood; not only dangerous, such 'hierarchical claims to the inherent originality or 'purity' of cultures are untenable', too (p37). This is why Bhabha insists on the neologism, 'DissemiNation', which emphasises that nations are '*internally* marked by the discourses of minorities, the heterogeneous histories of contending peoples, antagonistic authorities and tense locations of cultural difference' (p148). In other words, not only Hepzibah and Johnny but the child refugees, too, are seen to have an impact on the Welsh community, just as did the English mine-owners, the slaves, and the Druids.

Bawden's novel is a complex work, and I have only really scraped its surface. What I have tried to do is show how the book destabilises a number of fixed categories: of gender, class, and nation – all of which are interlinked. But also, centrally, it troubles the adult-child binary. Using Bhabha's notion of hybridity, I have sought to show that the children's novel is an area where this uneasy relation, this tension, is frequently played out.

Bhabha's claim that '[t]he fantasy of the native is precisely to occupy the master's place while keeping his [sic] place in the slave's *avenging* anger' (p44) is something we find in many children's books, especially those of popular writers like Blyton and Dahl. But Bawden's novel is more subtle than most, in having the narrative itself stage this process. That is, although it concentrates on young Carrie and her peers, it also deals with their adult selves, through whose agency the children are/have been avenged. Knowledge of this state of affairs arrives like a prolepsis (a flash forward) although, in fact, it is the state of childhood that is really the flashback, the analepsis. In this way, adult and child categories are dislocated, and a general sense of in-betweenness is fostered, where identities 'are continually, *contingently*, 'opening out', remaking the boundaries' (Bhabha: 219). So, while adults might seek to colonise the child through 'children's literature', their ability to fix the child, let alone to secure the adult, remains remarkably tenuous.

Bibliography

Bawden, Nina (1973) *Carrie's War*. London: Gollancz

Bawden, Nina (1974) 'A Dead Pig and My Father' in *Children's Literature in Education,* 14, pp3-13

Bhabha, Homi K. (1994) *The Location of Culture.* London: Routledge, pp19-39, 40-65, 66-84, 85-92, 102-22, 139-70, 212-35

Nodelman, Perry (1992) 'The Other: Orientalism, Colonialism, and Children's Literature' in *Children's Literature Association Quarterly* 17, pp29-35

Paul, Lissa (1998) *Reading Otherways.* Stroud: Thimble Press

Rose, Jacqueline (1984) *The Case of Peter Pan, or the Impossibility of Children's Fiction.* London: Macmillan

Rudd, David (2004) 'The Conditions of Possibility of Children's Literature' in *The International Companion Encyclopedia of Children's Literature,* 2nd edition, Peter Hunt (ed.). London: Routledge

Said, Edward (1978) *Orientalism.* New York: Pantheon

Sinfield, Alan (1992) *Faultlines: Cultural Materialism and the Politics of Dissident Reading.* Oxford: Clarendon Press

Constructions of Childhood and Giorgio Agamben's *Infantia*

Katrien Vloeberghs

In the course of the eighteenth and nineteenth centuries, two paradigms in cultural history shaped the Western European concepts of child and childhood. On the one hand, Enlightenment thinking had a major influence on the vision of education as emancipation, as development toward a rational subject, as self-determination and active *bildung*. On the other hand, Romanticism, both as a continuation of the Enlightenment and as its major contestation, invoked and celebrated a cult of childhood as an innocent and uncorrupted shelter, as an object of nostalgic worship, as a state of being which is prone to the experience of the irrational and uncanny as well. Both contemporary theory and today's children's literature elaborate critical and selective reevaluations of the legacy of these constructions of childhood in Modernity: the legacy of the Enlightenment, its Romantic corrective and its sterile implementation during the bourgeois era.

The philosophical concept of *infantia*

Reflections on the condition and the image of childhood gain central importance through its intersection with two crucial issues in philosophical and literary theory today: the search for an alternative conceptualisation of temporality and the aftermath of the linguistic turn. Firstly, infancy and childhood have throughout modernity been regarded as a temporary stage which – depending on the ideological position the particular conceptualisation represents – has either to be successfully left behind in order to enter the much more desirable state of rational adulthood or productive citizenship, or the transience of which has to be considered as an irreversible and nostalgically deplored loss. In more recent modernist and postmodernist literary and theoretical figurations of childhood and infancy however, the spatial and temporal boundaries of the sphere of the infant and the child appear to be permeable. Numerous twentieth century philosophical thinkers and critics, such as Walter Benjamin, Hannah Arendt, Jean François Lyotard, Peter Sloterdijk, Julia Kristeva, and Giorgio Agamben stage the motif of the child and the figure of infancy, *infantia*, as concepts that transcend traditional linear chronology. Far from being merely a stage on the way to chronological or genealogical maturity, infancy is irrecuperably and indestructibly present and 'at work' regardless of age. In a second stance, the figuration of *infantia* in actual theory refers to an existential condition of speechlessness and is therefore linked to the experience of language beyond referential signification, to the (im)possibility of perception, subjectivity and community in a pre-linguistic condition.

In analysing the relationship between constructions of childhood on the one hand and philosophical and literary theory on the other hand, Agamben's conceptualisation of *infantia* is a particularly relevant case in point. The Italian philosopher and literary critic Giorgio Agamben whose theoretical writings have recently become highly influential both in Europe and in the United States because of the original way in which he combines critical theory and poststructuralism, proposes a theoretical configuration of infancy that radically innovates the philosophical significance of the concepts of child and childhood. While the figure of infancy plays a major role in Agamben's writing for decades, it is mainly in his more recent theoretical work that he carries its traditional sociocultural and philosophical meaning beyond its existing horizon. Throughout his writings, Agamben takes up and critically transforms the two dominant narratives of growing up and development in modern Western culture, namely the Enlightenment and Romanticism. He enriches and transcends these two discourses with facets of twentieth century thought that have their offspring in Nietzsche and Freud and draws a concept of infancy that designs the possibility of an alternative experience of temporality and history, of subjectivity and language.

In many ways, Agamben's investment of the notion of infancy is close to the recent theoretical configurations of infancy in the writings of contemporary thinkers such as Jean François Lyotard and Julia Kristeva. These current constructions of childhood in philosophical writing and literary theory endow the concept of infancy with an anarchic dimension, with a genuine power of resistance against smooth integration into a linear development, subject formation and the symbolic order. Encountering the a-historical and anamnetic, pre-subjective, speechless condition of *infantia*, the human subject or individual is instantaneously confronted with the artificiality and therefore the ultimate vulnerability of crucial dimensions in human life and society. Infancy and childhood remind of the constructedness of both the linear and cyclical model of temporal continuity, of the individual as a socialised, integrated subject, and of the arbitrary nature of linguistic references in discourse. Agamben's conceptualisation of infancy and childhood however distinguishes itself from Lyotard's and Kristeva's figurations by endowing the potentiality of infancy with a surprising utopian dimension, more specifically a messianic potential. The evolution of this messianic idea in Agamben's depiction of infancy shows in an exemplary way how today's constructions of childhood creatively use and transform the Enlightened and Romantic paradigms. An analysis of Agamben's texts 'The Idea of Infancy' (1989) and *Infancy and History* (2000) against the background of Modernity's constructions of childhood indicates that the concept of infancy is currently in full evolution and may be entering a new stage.

Infantia as specificity of mankind

In 'The Idea of Infancy', Agamben draws an unexpected parallel between, on the one hand, the case of an albino salamander in Mexico's fresh water lakes which appears to hold on to its foetal characteristics instead of going through the normal metamorphosis in order to develop into an adult specimen, and, on the other, the development of humankind in general and each newborn human in particular. In his highly original narrative of ontogenesis, the specificity of the human manifests itself in 'neoteny' or 'pedomorphosis', concepts which refer to the biological phenomenon of evolutionary fixation. Thereby, a set of characteristics that are temporary in the development of primates are maintained throughout the onto- as well as phylogenesis of the human. In Agamben's view this specificity:

> explain[s] those morphological characteristics of man, ranging from the position of the occipital orifice to the form of the auricle of the ear, and from his hairless skin to the structure of his hands and feet, which do not correspond to those of adult anthropoids, but to those of the foetus (1989: 96).

Thus, for Agamben, the specificity of mankind is obviously not situated in those characteristics which distinguish man from primates in the sense that they have reached a higher stage of development. Instead, he marks the presence of an irrecuperable infancy as that which distinguishes mankind from all other living beings and which enables the human's entering into history, subjectivity and language.

Agamben's rather pseudo-scientific hypothesis sheds a surprising and disturbing light on one of the central assumptions in Modernity's constructions of childhood. The age old parallelism between the development of the individual child and the development of mankind as a whole, the analogy between phylo- and ontogenesis has traditionally been linked to a teleological and progressive shape and dynamic. Although Agamben echoes the traditional analogy, his thesis subversively transforms it into an alternative theory of evolution. His surprising narrative construction of the development of mankind as, in truth, a form of evolutionary regression, formulates a critique of the Enlightenment idea of progressive continuity and linear development (*Entwicklung*) on the one hand and of the Romantic, to some extent deterministic conception of harmonious deployment (*Entfaltung*) on the other. Both linear progress in Enlightenment ideas and organic deployment in Romantic thinking support the conceptualisation of development as a potential to be actualised as a systematic and controllable temporal continuity. Agamben's theory of infancy picks up, yet opposes these traditional conceptualisations both through an alternative understanding of potentiality and through a particular transformation of the habitual understanding of temporality. He argues how infancy transcends its temporal boundaries and ungraspably continues to haunt all subsequent stages of life or history. Within this topology, infancy assumes the position of a liminal caesura, marking the transition from a-historicity to historicity, from pre-subjectivity to subjectivity and from speechlessness to language. This transition is critical and holds a subversive potential: the operations to go from one mode of being to the other, the processes of growing up, developing a proper subjectivity, making the entry into the symbolic order inevitably entail a rebellious and disruptive residue. That what refuses to be integrated and insists on the fissure between opposite poles is conceptualised in Agamben's theory as a rest of negative or existing potentiality.

Liminal potentiality

For his conceptualisation of potentiality and actuality, which are crucial elements in his philosophy in general and his conception of infancy in particular, Agamben draws on the Aristotelian distinction between generic and existing potentiality. Unlike the '*generic potentiality*', which can manifest itself only in the actualisation through, for example, a learning process or a biologically determined transformation, the '*existing potentiality*' is 'a potentiality that is not simply the potential to do this or that thing but potential to not-do, potential not to pass into actuality.' (1999: 179-180) Although generic potentiality has traditionally been associated with the sphere of childhood, Agamben, in his attempt to grasp the specificity of infancy, clearly favours the other option, the negative or existing potentiality.

In 'The Idea of Infancy', the comparison with the salamander who clutches to its larval existence throughout its life time makes clear how the force of infancy is associated with a negative potentiality, with the freedom to refuse to develop, with the playful rebellion against the idea of progress and perfection through the conscious and wilful choice for a particular language, a specific culture, a particular tradition. This maintenance of the original openness is explicitly linked to the resistance to become an adult, whereas traditionally, specific cultural efforts are considered to aim at staving off the threat of evolutionary fixation, the abysmal openness of eternal infant potentiality:

The plurality of nations and the numerous historical languages are the false callings by which man attempts to respond to his intolerable absence of voice; or, if one prefers, they are the attempts, fatally come to nothing, to make graspable the ungraspable, to become – this eternal child – an adult. (1989: 98)

From this perspective, traditional conceptualisations of *Entwicklung* and *Entfaltung*, of development and deployment, are both driven by an ultimately doomed and self-destructive striving towards completion and totality. The particular actualisation of an open potential during the process of growing up of an individual or during the development of a particular society does not signify a further step in maturation or in mankind's perfectibility, but on the contrary blocks off the access to infant, i.e. existing/negative potentiality. Similarly, *infantia* does not participate in the harmonious, naturally successive stages of deployment of the generic potentiality always already inherent in its origins or beginnings. Infancy maintains a state of undetermined openness, emptiness and instability, which manifests itself in the permeability of infancy's temporal boundaries and its affinity with a liminal topology.

The power of infancy to undo stultifying oppositions between regression and progression and to explode its own temporal boundaries, is attributed by Agamben to its liminal topology. Infancy's capacity to assume a liminal and impure position between two opposite poles and to simultaneously enable their bridging and point out their fissure, marks the critical caesura which keeps alive an indeterminacy and an open potentiality. In various texts by Agamben, figurations of *infantia* refer to a threefold liminality: on the level of temporality, of subjectivity and of representation through language. *Infantia* becomes the name for the place and the moment where the synchrony of cyclical and mythical time and the diachrony of linear time meet and install the possibility of historicity. However, it also simultaneously designates the residue of that encounter, a residue that is constituted by liminal reminiscences of an impurity which cannot be integrated into the experience of time as either a detached synchronic moment or as a diachronic and linear continuum. Subsequently, Agamben argues how the volatile and unexpected confrontation with traces of the infant in play or memory has the uncanny power to destabilise the distinction between subject and object. The encounter evokes an experience of the self and the world in that twilight zone where the state of being of the self is neither dominated by symbiotic oneness with the environment nor by clearcut boundaries of the subject. In a third stance, infancy signifies the liminal caesura, the critical moment which installs and reminds of the constitutive fissure between pure potential language and actual discourse, between what Agamben calls the semiotic materiality of language and its symbolic referentiality. In its liminality, infancy embodies the 'potentiality not to', the potential to avoid, to refuse providing the link between the opposite spheres. As such, it can disturb and block the historical organisation of society, the formation of the subject and the initiation into language.

Agamben's messianic child

In his explicit celebration of infancy's redemptive force to render traditional temporal and spatial frameworks permeable, Agamben goes one step further than previous figurations of infancy in contemporary theory. His not unproblematic radicality stands out even more visibly against the background of two constants in the construction of child and childhood in Western cultural history. The (dis)continuity of development and the presence of a redemptive potential are two recurring elements in pointing out the interconnectedness between the idea of childhood and the conceptualisation of history.

Firstly, at the latest from the beginning of western Modernity, the figure of the child has been instrumentalised as a metaphor that either ensures or disturbs the continuity of historical development and the possibility to represent history as a homogeneous meta-narrative. Whereas the dominant eighteenth and nineteenth century conceptualisations of infancy and childhood locate them as primary stages that keep the promise of further continuous development, modernist, and even more so postmodernist figurations, heavily indebted to the theoretical framework of psychoanalysis, stress the disruptive and regressive forces of encounters with infancy and childhood. Agamben's description of the human as 'neotenic infant' however provides the onto- and phylogenetic regression with a potential of progression, and thereby creates a third position made out of a combination of these two different strands in conceptualisations of infancy and childhood.

Secondly, the attribution of a redemptive potential to the infant appears to be inherent in the linking of the conception of child and that of history. In the two dominant narratives of childhood and growing up, Enlightenment and Romanticism, which are each characterised by an articulate philosophy of history, the motif of infancy embodies elements that point to the utopian beginning and/or final resting point of the continuum depicting the development of the human individual and of mankind as such. Although highly critical of totalitarian visions of a utopian future as well as of a homogeneous historical narrative, twentieth century literature and theory surprisingly continue to activate this association between the figure of the child and the potential of redemption. In a tradition grounded in Nietzsche, the condition of *infantia* stands for an ideal and utopian final destination of humankind which can only be reached precisely when the concept of progressive development is given up. With his figuration of infancy, Giorgio Agamben situates himself in this tradition. He envisages an alternative utopian idea which no longer stands for some final resting point that is to be reached and upon which all movement will stand still, but rather as the eventual actualisation of a potentially permanent renewal. Just like Nietzsche's motif of the child in *Thus Spoke Zarathustra*, Agamben's *infantia* effectuates through its play a dynamic that resists a fixed beginning and closure and embodies an a-historical, a-memorial condition, 'entrusted to oblivion' (1989: 97). In a radical and in some respect questionable step, Agamben saves and transforms the utopian potential derived from traditional narratives of childhood, and envisions messianic redemption, a coming community, a 'royaume enfantin'.

Infantia and children's literature

A comparison between *infantia*'s function in two texts marks a significant shift, and simultaneously links up to an insight into the specific potential of (children's) literature. Whereas the characteristics of infancy – its potentiality, its liminality as spatial and temporal caesura – remain constant throughout his work, the function of infancy's potential shifts from a stabilising and integrative component to an emphasis on the infant's disruptive force as well as its redemptive power.

The essay 'Le Pays des Jouets – Réflections sur L'histoire et sur le Jeu' in Agamben's early work *Infancy and History* (1978) is dedicated to Claude Lévi-Strauss and undertakes an attempt to carry his stucturalist-anthropologist insights further. This text marks most clearly the function of infancy to ensure the continuity of the social system and the circle of life. Agamben draws a parallel between two groups of beings, 'unstable signifiers' (p105), which are both characterised by a liminality that bridges the fundamental opposition between the world of the living and that of the dead, and at the same time renders the dichotomic organisation of society and history impure. Agamben evokes the example of the threatening presence of the ghosts of recently defunct people, semi-dead beings, which necessitates a funeral rite to be executed in order to direct them securely to the sphere of the dead and the forefathers. Similarly, newborn infants, semi-living beings, ask for a mediating ritual of initiation which undoes their dangerous and unstable ambiguity and turns them without residue into full humans, inhabitants of the world of the living. At this early stage of Agamben's thinking about infancy, the function of liminal creatures in general, and of the infant in particular, still carries traces of an ultimately stabilising dynamic of integration and continuation of the system. However, the more recent text 'The Idea of Infancy' questions both the desirability and the possibility of such fixation and recuperation. It is striking that Agamben, in envisioning the conditions for the coming of the messianic age, emphasises the disruptive force of infancy. Seemingly contradictory, the radical interruption of continuity is connected to and considered to be a precondition to reach the end of this history and tradition. Agamben crucially distinguishes his conceptualisation of infancy's redemptive potential from any kind of utopian totality or wholeness and situates the messianic moment precisely in discontinuity, enhanced by infancy's perpetual potentiality and impure liminality.

As argued above, the discursive and argumentative part of 'Le Pays des Jouets - Réflections sur L'histoire et sur le Jeu' emphasises the necessity of integration and continuation. In his literary reference to Collodi's children's classic *Pinocchio* and the author's legendary description of the infantile utopia, however, this early text already prefigures *infantia*'s rebellious and revolutionary questioning of the *status quo*. It is significant that Agamben's *infantia* first gains contours on the foil of a children's classic, and against the background of ample reference to the semantic field of child, childhood and – most crucially – the child's play. Indeed, the more recent text 'The Idea of Infancy' clearly states that 'it is [the child's] *play* ... which keeps ajar that never setting openness' (p98). Is this 'Pays des Jouets' maybe to be reached after a night's travel on a speaking donkey? What will we find 'when time has come to fullness' (p98)? Will it be a redeemed society in which the supremacy of history, subjectivity and the symbolic order surrenders to a universe of jingling toys and a vertiginous acceleration of time, in which the calendar is rendered superfluous, together with the adult desire to be a real boy and to master the book of ABC?

Bibliography

Agamben, Giorgio (1989) 'Idée de l'Enfance' in *Idée de la Prose*, Christian Bourgeois (ed.). Paris: Presses Bretoliennes, pp81-86.

Agamben, Giorgio (1999) 'Potentialities' in *Collected Essays in Philosophy*, Daniel Heller-Roazen (ed.). Stanford: Stanford University Press

Agamben, Giorgio (2000) 'Enfance et Histoire. Essai sur la Destruction de L'Expérience' in *Enfance et Histoire*, Giorgio Agamben (ed.) Paris: Edition Payot, p17-82, 83-109

Storytelling and the Adult/Child Relationship in Geraldine McCaughrean's *A Pack of Lies*, or the Dilemma of Children's Fiction

Virginie Douglas

Attempts have been made to examine the specificity of children's literature by studying the differences in point of view, tone and address when the implied reader is an adult and when (s)he is a child. In *The Narrator's Voice*, whose subtitle *The Dilemma of Children's Fiction* I have borrowed for this article, Barbara Wall asserts that 'adults ... speak differently in fiction when they are aware that they are addressing children.' (1991: 2-3) One of the main features of children's literature is that it is based on an insolvable paradox, which Zohar Shavit, in an article, calls 'The Double Attribution of Texts for Children':

> By definition, children's literature addresses children, but always and without exception, children's literature has an additional addressee - the adult, who functions as either a passive or an active addressee of texts written for children.' (1999: 83)

And indeed the very ambiguity of the genitive in the phrase 'children's books/literature' is a significant sign of this paradox. Does children's literature belong to children at all? How can an author address a young reader using the right words and conveying the right point of view when (s)he has long forgotten what it is to be a child? What do we (adults) mean when we say that children appropriate certain books? Contemporary children's literature is well aware of the essential inadequacy on which children's books are based and is not content with comfortably writing down to the child as it used to do. On the contrary it has recently explored and exploited this dilemma.

Although the effects of adult intervention into children's literature can be analysed at any of the stages of the creation and marketing of a book, in the literary perspective adopted by this paper, it is narration which crystallises the adult author/child reader paradox most clearly. In his preface to the adult edition of *The Daydreamer*, an unclassifiable book published at once in an edition for adults and an edition for children (illustrated by Anthony Browne) and categorised either as a novel or a collection of stories, Ian McEwan points out this dilemma inherent to children's fiction, by showing that in the process of writing a children's book, both the adult telling the story and the child narratee are constructs rather than actual individuals:

> I became more than usually attentive to the sound of an adult voice speaking each sentence. This adult was not, or not simply, me. Alone

> in my study, I read aloud passages to an imaginary child (not quite, or not only, one of mine) on behalf of this imaginary adult. (1995: 7)

The child reader especially is elusive, being a complex combination of real children (the author's own or others), the child the author remembers – or thinks (s)he remembers – (s)he used to be and the ideal child (s)he would like to address. Acknowledging the fundamental 'impossibility of children's fiction', McEwan says that he eventually resolved 'to write a book for adults about a child in a language that children could understand' (p9), thus resorting to dual address in order to make up for his inability, as an adult, to write adequately for a child reader.

Geraldine McCaughrean's novel *A Pack of Lies* (1988), which received both the Carnegie Medal and the *Guardian* Children's Fiction Award, is one example that illuminates the dilemma of children's fiction: by putting forward a two-sided stance regarding the process of storytelling, her text epitomizes this basic paradox. McCaughrean's gift for storytelling has often been praised, and indeed her books are first and foremost stories told to a child narratee from a very traditional adult-narrator stance. Before writing stories of her own, she published numerous, acclaimed retellings of texts from all periods of history and from all over the world having achieved a mythical status, including Greco-Roman mythology, English legend and even literary classics. Drawing on all kinds of oral and written literature has been an unvarying feature of children's books ever since the development of children's literature in the second half of the eighteenth century, after the London publisher John Newbery started selling books which were addressed to children and included a large range of texts from folklore. In this respect McCaughrean's works are in keeping with what is commonly referred to as the best tradition of children's literature. Even when she started publishing original novels with *A Little Lower than the Angels*, McCaughrean went on making use of the repertoire she had explored in her retellings, basing her plots on characters directly borrowed from folklore and adopting the style of highly-coded subgenres. As a result, her novels clearly endorse a conventional vision of the kind of adult/child relationship that is established through storytelling. By telling a captivating story, the author assumes the persona of a reliable storyteller, whose respect of conventions, omniscience and superiority guarantee a relationship based on trust but also on the creation of literary illusion, in other words on unilateral communication from writer to reader.

In this respect, *A Pack of Lies* can be construed as a digest of the whole of McCaughrean's production for children. A mysterious man who calls himself MCC Berkshire offers to work for nothing (except board and lodging and the permission to read books) at the antique dealer's shop of Mrs Povey, Ailsa's mother; he succeeds in selling one piece of furniture or trinket after another, thus saving the business from bankruptcy, by telling the customers the supposed stories of these objects. In fact the greatest part of the novel consists of the stories told by MCC and embedded within the main narrative. Despite the complex narrative frame, the twelve stories which make up the novel are delivered in their entirety, without any interruption, by a reassuring or, on the contrary, alarmingly reproving, at any rate patronising narrator to an entranced intradiegetic audience of customers and a supposedly equally spellbound extradiegetic public of young readers.

Each chapter includes a prologue in which MCC meets and sizes up his audience before announcing he is going to tell a story, thus inviting the listeners to make themselves comfortable: '[the customer] tucked his fingers together on the crown of his waistcoated stomach, sat back and listened to the story MCC had to tell.' (p14) The transition between the main narrative frame and the embedded stories is delineated by a space in the typographical layout so that the different narrative levels should not be confused. The twelve tales (each having its own title under the chapter headings, such as 'The Clock: A Story of Superstition') could in fact be extracted from the novel and make up a separate collection of stories. What the reader is given to witness here is the staging of the relationship between the narrator and the narratees as it is enacted through storytelling, the strong presence of these two agencies being traditionally considered as a prerequisite of children's fiction. MCC acts as the intrusive narrator of children's books, a narrator who is meant to reproduce comfortable, reassuring social or family patterns through the bond created thanks to storytelling. It is even hinted that MCC's presence is consoling in the sense that he conveniently replaces Ailsa's late father, Mrs Povey having been recently widowed, as if some authority were conferred on him within the family circle by his mere authorship or indeed by his mere voice: in chapter 11, Ailsa is moved to tears when, from her bedroom, she hears her mother and MCC talking together after dinner just as her parents used to do.

The setting up of a relationship based on trust therefore makes it possible for the narrator, once the telling of the story has started, to generate literary illusion and keep his audience engrossed. Only a small part of MCC's intradiegetic audience are actually children (young Ailsa is always present during the storytelling sessions and one of the customers is a girl, whose parents want to buy her a present, but all the others are adults); and yet the narratees repeatedly seem to be infantilised by the process of storytelling, a process which is itself presented as relevant to children's literature: 'Ailsa thought for a moment that the telephone engineer had fallen asleep, as children do who are read to at night.' (p74) The storyteller becomes a figure of authority who has no difficulty in intoxicating the narratee, explicitly compared with a child, with his words, thus holding him in his power.

Hence children's literature, insofar as it is equated with storytelling, involves the supremacy of the adult author/narrator figure in his relationship with the child (or childlike) addressees. But the link between the stories provided by the storyteller figure of MCC, which turns the collection of unrelated stories into a novel (the subtitle is 'Twelve Stories in One'), is too much elaborated upon to aim only at acknowledging that the book belongs to children's literature. McCaughrean makes the character of MCC intriguing enough for the reader – and, in the diegesis, for Ailsa – to want to learn more about him and wonder whether he has no other function than just telling comfortable stories to a motley series of customers.

Significantly, MCC himself is a highly literary character, a character made of paper and words. The first time he is mentioned, Ailsa sees him reflected on the screen of a microfiche machine, with his face superimposed with the words of the document she has been reading. In addition, the whiteness of the cricket trousers he invariably wears and whose grass stains are an imprint of his recent history evokes the blank page which is to be written on. Like an inscribable surface, an unwritten book, MCC is neutral, open to all possibilities. The few elements we learn about his identity seem to be suggested to him by the circumstances and made up as he goes along. In his article 'Only Make-Believe? Lies, Fictions, and Metafictions in Geraldine McCaughrean's *A Pack of Lies* and Philip Pullman's *Clockwork*', Dudley Jones (1999) goes over the mysterious character's playful particulars: the initials of his first name are the same which stand for the prestigious Marylebone Cricket Club, while his surname, Berkshire, is consistent with the fact that he claims he comes from Reading, presumably meaning the main city in this county but which, if you take it literally as suggested by the character's incorrect pronunciation of '*Reading* to rhyme with 'breeding'' (p4), reinforces the man's literariness.

It then becomes obvious that while he occasionally appears as a patronising, unambiguous storyteller, MCC also plays the role of a metafictive agent in the novel. As the provider of the stories, he offers a reflexive stance on the act of storytelling. The screen of the microfiche machine, a modernised version of Alice's mirror, may be the best metaphor of this self-reflexivity, as the words covering the reflection of MCC Berkshire's face are titles of books, printed upside down and inside out (because of Ailsa's failure to use the machine correctly) in a typographical game reminiscent of Carroll's 'Jabberwocky' poem, among which are the very title, publisher and date of McCaughrean's novel. The move that the child reader is obliged to make, standing in front of a mirror with the book in his hands, if he wants to decipher the cryptic words corresponds to the active approach he is encouraged to favour in his reading of the novel. The image of the mirror is further developed in chapter 8, 'The Mirror: A Story of Vanity', where a vain girl is dragged into the reversed world of a mirror by her own reflection, who then takes her place in the diegesis: beyond the narcissistic self-consciousness offered by the mirror, the universe glimpsed 'through the looking-glass' suggests a world of fiction awaiting – indeed calling for – exploration. The adult/child relationship is no longer one involving a cosy merging of the young addressee with the storyteller: it implies a new distance represented by the screen of the microfiche machine, a questioning attitude bringing about the awareness of how narration works behind the scenes. MCC gets through one of the central notions of the novel, referred to in its title, both to Ailsa and to the child reader who can identify with her: when accused of being a liar, he states (thus ruining his own effort at creating literary illusion) that the real world should not be confused with the diegetic world and that his stories are not 'lies' but 'fiction', which does not exclude truth (p24).

The first element of doubt regarding storytelling is to be found in the very nature and variety of the hypotexts explored by McCaughrean thanks to the stories told by MCC. There is almost something overdone in the wide range of periods and backgrounds in which the tales are set, and the resort to cultural contexts exterior to the Western civilization (one story is set in India while another takes place in China) raises the question of the extent of the narrator's reliability. Admittedly, as far as background is concerned, MCC researches his stories as any good novelist does (he is recurrently shown to have been reading a book having the same context or belonging to the same genre as the story he tells), but on balance his knowledge is – like the books in Povey's antiquary – second-hand.

Moreover, by drawing on the codes and conventions of specific genres and subgenres, *A Pack of Lies* reaches a point when by overusing them, the novel subverts them. In an essay entitled 'Children's, Adult, Human . . . ?', Maria Nikolajeva (1999) convincingly notes that children's fiction is characterised by its 'clear-cut generic features' and that '[n]o mixing of genres is acknowledged in children's novels, mainly for pedagogical purposes: supposedly, children wish to know from the start what kind of story they are dealing with.' She goes on to show that 'genre eclecticism, most notably the blending of 'high' and 'low' genres', which is now often to be found in adult fiction, is still unusual in children's fiction, where it therefore becomes a challenge to conventions (p65). In *A Pack of Lies*, the mere bringing together of stories belonging to various (sub)genres calls the canons of children's literature into question. The undermining of the storytelling process is carried further by the deriding of these subgenres, especially the most characteristically codified among them, through the play on the clichés and conventions they use. This is particularly obvious in the wild comedy of the supposed whodunnit, with its grossly incompetent inspector, and of the alleged Gothic story, where horror turns into farce through its sheer excess. Literature is debunked, divested of its mythical aura. The reader is bluntly reminded that, all things considered, stories are nothing but commodities and that literature is only business, as is made clear in MCC's use of stories as an incentive to convince the customers to spend their money.

By telling these stories strewn with elements of self-mockery, MCC encapsulates the dilemma of children's fiction. On the one hand, he endorses the patronising function of conventional children's books: this function expresses itself through the collusion and bringing together of the child narratee and the authoritative yet pampering adult storyteller, whose status embraces and deliberately confuses the two separate agencies of author and narrator. On the other hand, thanks to the thought-provoking effect of his elusiveness, MCC plays a disrupting role, which creates a tension between the child addressee and the superior adult but at the same time forces the former into maturity. The adult/child opposition of traditional children's fiction then becomes obliterated, and the child is treated as an equal or at least as a mature person worthy of being introduced to the procedures of narration. MCC is in turn irritatingly omnipresent or absent when he is needed, disappearing only to turn up again unexpectedly. This game of hide-and-seek between narrator and narratees clearly dissociates the mysterious storyteller from the conventional monolithic, infallible narrator figure of children's books.

The characteristically post modern metafictional nature of McCaughrean's text, which Jones examines in his study of the novel, exemplifies a new kind of didacticism at work in some recent children's fiction, which aims at emancipating the child through the calling into question of the storytelling process and the undermining of the traditional adult/child bond in relation with narration. *A Pack of Lies* is one of the books which best illustrate the move from the long-established, conformist didacticism (aimed at social integration) of children's books to a new, subversive kind of pedagogy, whose purpose is to teach critical distance through the questioning of all values, certainties and norms. Admittedly the novel provides moral lessons in the tradition of children's literature: most of the embedded stories can be read as cautionary tales, warning the narratees against sins (among which some of the deadly sins), which are explicitly pinpointed in the subtitles of the stories (for example: 'The Table: A Story of Gluttony'; or, 'The Lead Soldier: A Story of Pride'). Moral values certainly pervade the whole novel, and are presented as being far more important than material value in the story 'The Plate: A Question of Values', where a Chinese girl chooses to give up a valuable plate for her lover's sake.

Yet the main lessons conveyed by the novel may not be the more evident ones. Thanks to its interlocking narrative frames (mainly put into perspective in the first and the last chapters) and its mise-en-abyme of the storytelling process, the novel explores anew such – apparently – obvious notions as what makes a book, what makes a novel, what makes an author or what makes a child. Through the figure of MCC, McCaughrean draws red herrings across the young reader's trail so as to have him unravel the intricacies of fiction. The reader has to go beyond the two-fold pattern of narrator versus narratees, in parallel with the adult/child antagonism, to be faced with a series of half overlapping agencies which include the deliberately blurred concepts of narrator, narratee, character, author and reader.

Within the diegesis, the existence of MCC is gradually questioned. Ailsa, who is aware of MCC's literariness and want of history, origins and family, suspects that he might be a fictional character just like the characters in his own stories. He actually seems to be made of the same literary matter as the stories he reads: one of the books he has been reading is said to be 'the exact colour and texture of MCC Berkshire's shoes' (p164), while another book 'had a green, cloth-bound cover' (p162) reminiscent of the storyteller's green corduroy jacket (this last word also applying to books). Besides, when the book with the green cover is opened by Ailsa at the beginning of the last chapter, it reveals its title, *The Man Who Came From Reading*, the very title of the novel's first chapter and, in an indented paragraph, the description of a man, a passage directly taken from the physical portrait of MCC in the same chapter. This equation of MCC with a fictional character seems corroborated by the fact that he claims he comes from Reading, meaning the reading of books, since he first appears in the library and seems to be returning there when Ailsa last sees him.

However, McCaughrean goes further in a fragmentation of the storyteller figure which invalidates any possibility of imposing a unique, one-way interpretation on the child. Indeed, in an ironical twist, a final mise-en-abyme of the whole novel, the last chapter brings a new possible 'reading' of MCC's many-sided personality. Mrs Povey and her daughter suddenly realise (although this interpretation is only very subtly suggested) that, despite his shiftiness, all along MCC has been not only the narrator of the embedded stories but the author of the main narrative itself and therefore their own creator. The last three pages of the novel tell us more about Michael Charles Christie Berkshire, depicting him in an unfavourable light, now that he no longer benefits from the appealing looks his fictional status endowed him with. This realistic effect aiming at presenting MCC Berkshire as the real author of *A Pack of Lies* (when the novelist's elderly mother sees the title of the manuscript on his desk, she drops it into the bin disapprovingly) is reinforced by the presence of some autobiographical elements which further blur the different agencies at work: it seems to me that the initials MCC, in addition to referring to a famous cricket club, bear an interesting resemblance to the beginning of McCaughrean's surname; it should also be stressed that the novelist lives in Berkshire and that her daughter is called

Ailsa, even if 'Ailsa Povey', the imperfect anagram of *A Pack of Lies*, rather seems to place the girl on the side of fiction.

Finally renouncing the authority conferred on him by his auctorial status, MCC decides to enter the fictional world he has created and live there. Through authorship, the authority of adults in the process of narration and in general is challenged. Laying responsibilities on the child reader when classic children's literature tended to maintain him in an infantile state reverses the traditional pattern of adult/child relationships as they are enacted in children's books. Revealingly the adults in McCaughrean's novel often seem more childish than the only major child character, Ailsa. Mrs Povey's inefficiency and inability to provide for the needs of her small family come close to irresponsibility. As for MCC, his power as a storyteller is counterbalanced by a childlike tendency to live from day to day, which is emphasised by the question of his mysterious age:

> ... Ailsa looked at him and wondered how old he was. Generally speaking the world could be dealt, like a pack of cards, into two stacks — people like her mother and people like her — with a few miscellaneous babies and old people on the discard pile. Try as she might, she could not put an age to Mr Berkshire. He was much older than her, of course, but far younger than her mother. In fact there did not seem to be enough years between her age and her mother's age to fit in all the ages MCC Berkshire might be. (p121)

Thanks to his agelessness, the author figure is seen as the mediator of the withdrawal of the age barrier between adults and children, the generation gap being now seen as an outdated, irrelevant concept. The presence, in the recent output of children's books, of novels which revise the old adult/child dialectic (the pack of cards neatly dealt into two stacks) may contribute, in future decades, to the dying out – or at least the absorption into mainstream literature – of the specific literary category called 'children's books'.

Bibliography

Jones, Dudley (1999) 'Only Make-Believe? Lies, Fictions, and Metafictions in Geraldine McCaughrean's *A Pack of Lies* and Philip Pullman's *Clockwork*' in *The Lion and the Unicorn,* 23, 1, January, pp86-96

McCaughrean, Geraldine (1988) *A Pack of Lies.* Oxford: Oxford University Press

McEwan, Ian (1995) *The Daydreamer.* London: Vintage

Nikolajeva, Maria (1999) 'Children's, Adult, Human ...?' in *Transcending Boundaries. Writing for a Dual Audience of Children and Adults*, Sandra L. Beckett (ed.). New York: Garland, pp63-80

Rose, Jacqueline (1984) *The Case of Peter Pan, or the Impossibility of Children's Fiction*. London: Macmillan

Shavit, Zohar (1999) 'The Double Attribution of Texts for Children and How It Affects Writing for Children' in *Transcending Boundaries. Writing for a Dual Audience of Children and Adults*, Sandra L. Beckett (ed.). New York: Garland, pp83-97

Wall, Barbara (1991) *The Narrator's Voice: The Dilemma of Children's Fiction*. London: Macmillan

Who is the Writer: The Child or the Adult?

Maiko Miyoshi

In many children's books, there are characters who get involved in the act of writing. The forms this writing takes are diverse, including genres such as diaries, journals, letters, stories and autobiography. The images of young characters who clearly show their thoughts and emotions in this way are very powerful, as when these children reveal joy, show anger, ask questions and express wishes and hopes, at the same time, they imply their autonomy. This pattern, of characters who write, has been on the increase since the 1960s, probably in tandem with the rise of special realism in literature. Parallel to it has been an increase in the use of first person narrative, which is examined by some critics (Wall, 1991; Nikolajeva, 2002: 223-267). However, there is no study focusing on characters who are writing, or on the spread of employing such a pattern as a phenomenon, in spite of the complexity it often involves. Its use fosters features such as reality, intimacy, reflexivity and symbolism, which tends to reveal politic contradictions between adult and child. Regarding these characteristics, this paper explores the significance of this pattern, how it functions, why it is used so often in children's literature, why it is increasing significantly, and, finally, what it means in present-day society. Most significantly, in relation to the above-mentioned functions, this pattern generates a range of self-identities. These relate to the society where these books are written and read, a society which anticipates variations in the understanding of self-identity. Meanwhile, as my title suggests, the question 'Who is the *real* writer?' examines the ideal image of fictional child writers and reveals adult authors of the texts, thus suggesting the complex power relationship between children and adults in a broad context. These issues simultaneously indicate the complexity and possibilities of this pattern.

Before specifying the characters who are writing, it is significant to study the general images of child figures who by writing conduct some kind of enunciation of their role and function. Generally speaking, the issue of voice plays a significant role for appreciation and interpretation of literature, and critics, for example Barbara Wall, mention that 'the nature of that voice, and the way it speaks within the text, is of primary importance in assessing fiction for children' (1991: 272). Aidan Chambers observes that '[t]one of voice, style as a whole, very quickly establishes a relationship between author and reader' (1985: 98). Child figures with their own voices seem to be innovative, affirmative and welcoming in children's literature, where adults have traditionally been associated with pedagogical and moralistic messages and controls. Furthermore, as a narrative device and technique, first person narrative has become the most effective way to represent children's own voices. Andrea Schwenke Wyile (1999) analyses first-person narration, and shows the patterns and effects that first-person narrative generates by means of focalisation. Its intimacy and immediacy create reality, plausibility as well as irony, and raise questions for readers. The word 'engagement' is one of the key words in this author's study, and it implies that the connection between readers and writers becomes the most significant issue. This relationship is especially problematic, since most children's books are written, produced, and sold by adults, whilst the first-person narration still gives an impression that they are the voices of child characters. Therefore it seems to reverse the usual formula that writers and adults are superior to readers and children.

The relationship between children and adults is also, significantly, related to the issue of the status of the reader, which is mainly numerically dominated by children in the realm of children's literature. Perhaps, due to the impact of poststructualism in mainstream literature, and notions such as Barthes's 'The Death of the Author', (1987) the importance of the reader's involvement in reading is increasing. Also as J. A. Appleyard indicates, the influences of researchers with an educational faculty background, with knowledge of child psychology and pedagogical techniques (1991: 5) has enhanced the significance of the reader-orientated theory, especially in literature for children. The emphasis on readers also indicates the importance of perspective or point of view. This issue includes two aspects: the first is to give a specific perspective, which teaches children to have their own points of view, and see things from other perspectives. This encourages child readers to have understanding, compassion and tolerance towards others and eventually changes them from solipsists to a socially aware existence. This point seems to be especially relevant to contemporary society, where the diversity of people and of their value systems is rich. However, secondly, as Chambers argues, the issue of perspective shows what creates the author-reader relationship, as well as what forms the child reader into 'the kind of reader the book demands' (1990: 99), in order to convey the messages in the books fully and smoothly. Regarding this issue, Robyn McCallum summarises the genre of literature for young readers as 'a particular kind of discursive practice which is culturally situated and which constructs an implied audience position inscribed with the values and assumptions of the culture in which it is produced and received' (1999: 9). Thus, this would appear to prove that children's books, which seem on the one hand to be positively directed towards children, turn out not to be free from adults' intended or unintended manipulation, something which could be termed 'an ideological trap.'

In my research, the focus is more specifically on narratives written by fictional characters, such as letters, diaries, journals and autobiographies, all with first-person narrations. Within fiction containing such narrations, the following titles should be listed as examples; for younger readers, Louise

Fitzhugh's *Harriet the Spy* (1985), although this also includes third-person narrative, Beverly Cleary's *Dear Mr. Henshaw* (1983), Jacqueline Wilson's *The Story of Tracy Beaker* (1991), Sharon Creech's *Love That Dog* (2001), and for older readers, Robert O'Brien's *Z for Zachariah* (1987), Aidan Chambers's *Dance On My Grave* (1982), Berlie Doherty's *Dear Nobody* (1991), Jan Mark's *The Hillingdon Fox* (1991), Ted van Lieshout's *Brothers* (2001), David Almond's *Kit's Wilderness* (1999), Celia Rees's *Witch Child* (2000), and Janet Tashjian's *The Gospel: According to Larry* (2001).

These are very different from each other, and the voices and words of the characters do not necessarily function in the same way. However, these are more realistic styles than artificial monologues and unnatural addresses from characters to readers would be. This results from the practicality of the medium, since the imitation of real writing generates mimetic, thematic, and temporal functions, as Abbott (1984) suggests in his study of diary fiction. It is not the same thing to 'read' monologue such as the voice of Holden Caulfield in J.D. Salinger's *The Catcher in the Rye* (1994) rather than listening to it, as to 'read' writing, such as diaries and letters, which were intended to be read, in the first place.

One characteristic of these narrative accounts written by characters is its reflexivity, which, according to Anthony Giddens (1991: 76), leads to a self-interrogation. To question 'Who am I ?' is the essential step to knowing oneself and obtaining self-identity. Autobiography notwithstanding, many diaries and letters mainly deal with writers themselves; these writings cannot avoid being involved with the psychological phases experienced by the writers. Marilyn Chandler discusses the connection between the crisis in one's life and autobiography, and suggests the therapeutic function of writing autobiography. Furthermore, the point Linda Anderson and Laura Marcus make is significant when they state that, recently, letters, diaries and memoirs are achieving revaluation as 'private' or another kind of 'life writing' or autobiography in the light of feminist criticism (Anderson, 2001: 34 and Marcus, 1994: 81). Accordingly, fictional autobiography, diaries and letters may similarly represent writers who remember, reflect, think, consider, and imagine things in the past and the present while they write. In many cases, the story line involves many characters who write, achieving development and maturation for a better future at the end of each story. This may be interpreted as a common pattern in these texts, as well as an ideological image. These texts, compounded by the voices and words of writing personae, physically represent their progress as the stories proceed, every time readers turn the pages. These texts can be regarded as 'metafiction', defined as 'fiction which self-consciously draws attention to its status as text and as fictive' (McCallum, 1996: 397). The post modern aspect, which also includes multiple possibilities in perspectives, 'reflects the chaos and ambivalence of our life and the loss of absolute values and truths'

(Nikolajeva, 1996: 206), by interrogating the existences of both the books and the world the readers belong to.

It is very important to examine the point that adult authors of fiction and most child fictional characters equally use writing as their way of expressing themselves. In particular, when a number of novels suggest that writing characters produce creative and imaginative writing, as well as direct first person accounts of their thoughts and feelings, it seems to be that not only does this kind of fiction carry the identical image to that of the adult authors, but also represents the act of writing as having some symbolic image and significance, which function to indicate the independence and power of such writers in the fiction.

Incidentally, these fictional child writers seem to be almost equal to those children with pens in their hands in reality, whom McMaster celebrates for their ability, autonomy and authority:

> "The pen has been in your hands," Anne Elliot famously reminds a man, during a dispute in *Persuasion* about the relative virtues of the sexes. It is Jane Austen's most overtly feminist statement. The child, similarly, can with justice remind adults that the pen has been in their hands. The issue of who holds the pen is after all crucial. And when a child takes the pen in hand, that child is taking a determined step toward the control of language, of representation, of authority. The child, usually little, mostly subordinate, always subject to control by parent or baby-sitter or teacher, has a lot to gain by wresting the means of representation from the adults. (2001: 277)

This view about child writers is certainly based on reality and real people, and it may be irrelevant to compare it with the fictional characters who are writing in children's fiction. However, if this is the image of child writers, real or fictional, whatever they are, it is possible to interpret that the child characters who write in fiction are loaded with symbolic implications, as well as ideological images, in the first place.

In his study of masculinity in children's literature, John Stephens refers to the way of establishing subjectivity through writing experience, especially in the case of unconventional male characters, such as the New Age boy, whose:

> self-awareness often leads him to an understanding of how discourse shapes the world and hence to a realization that creativity is a form of agency, text production, whether as writing, imagining, or some other form, figures agential self-constitution (2000: 38).

This technique is certainly suitable for those who tend to have no place in society, but it is not necessarily limited to such minority cases. On the contrary, this scheme is appropriate for anybody, since it enables each individual to create his/her own subjectivity, instead of letting him/her have an unsuitable ready-made subjectivity imposed. In fact, the relation between the writing as act and the issues of agency, identity and self is examined further theoretically. In her study on connection between gender and agency, McNay explains the link between creativity, agency and act, stating that 'creative dimension to action is the condition of possibility of certain types of autonomous agency understood as the ability to act in an unexpected fashion or to institute new and unanticipated modes of behaviour' (2000: 22). This indicates that the act of writing simultaneously, proves the independence and sovereign power of the writers. Following McNay's argument, Stephens summarises:

> Narrative is the privileged medium of this process of self-formation. Insofar as coherent fictive subjects can be represented as engaged in an active process of making sense of the existents of story ... and the events which interact with those existents, they can be attributed with a capacity for self-formation and hence subjective agency. (2000: xii)

Thus, the writing figures in children's literature become the paradigm of maturation and development, with their performance of self-formation, through their writing experience. Paul Ricœur discusses the variations of identity, such as, 'self-constancy' and 'narrative identity', which can include 'change and mutability, within the cohesion of one lifetime.' (1985: 246). According to Ricœur, the latter case is also confirmed by study of autobiography, as 'the story of a life continues to be refigured by all the truthful or fictive stories a subject tells about himself or herself' (p246). At the same time, this view can be applied to children's fiction which takes the forms of fictive autobiography, diaries and letters. Therefore, the characters who write in these texts similarly project what Ricœur suggests, 'the self of self-knowledge' (p247). In his view, this is not the egotistical and narcissistic ego, but the fruit of an examined life, which owes much to cathartic narrative effects and culture. Furthermore, Ricœur suggests the possibility of application of narrative identity to a community, in addition to an individual. This gives another prospect in interpreting the texts for young readers, including characters who write: in other words, their narrative identities. Thus far, the focus has been placed on the issue of subjectivity, agency, and self-identity, which are obviously matters for the individual. However, at the same time, it may be possible to interpret that these characters who write represent the autonomous and powerful young people, which community and society today require.

Manipulation

So far, the argument has been focused on a number of functions, generated by the images of characters who write within the texts. These positive elements as literary technique, such as intimacy and plausibility, as well as powerful autonomous images, are suitable for creating positive and encouraging fiction, and therefore are beneficial for adult authors. On the other hand, when these are examined from the child readers' side, the familiar and intimate voices and words from their peers simply imply ideology or expectation. It may be too extreme and irrelevant a view, but they can even be regarded as giving subtle and indigenous propaganda, as well as misinformation. In that respect, these characters who write may seem to be puppets of the adult authors, who are acting as ventriloquists. Barbara Wall's in-depth study of narration indicates that many unsuccessful attempts to make child voices, including some cases of child writers, only reveal adult voices which are moralistic, didactic, ironic etc. John Stephens also suggests the first-person narration, including characters who write, 'turn[s] out to be no more than functions of narration' (2002: 39). These may imply that, to consider adult authors as ventriloquists, is too extreme, as well as being an unnecessary concern. However, Stephens also indicates the significance of pattern as, 'the site of enunciation offered by the mode of first-person narration, which came to dominate the literature during [the second half of the twentieth century], has seemed to guarantee an inner life and capacity for self-expression as images of subjectivity' (p39) so that the employment of these patterns should be examined more seriously.

Again regarding the image of ventriloquism, which is created by the coming together of adult authors of texts and fictional characters who write, in brief, writing as the medium of expressing themselves, becomes significant. The author of *Dumbstruck: A Cultural History of Ventriloquism*, Steven Connor, suggests the contradicting or binary nature of the ventriloquial voice, which mediates between 'body and language', and therefore between 'body and culture' (2003). According to Connor, the dissociated ventriloquial voice both challenges and reasserts the political authority, as it marks the self's presence as well as its estrangement from itself, at the same time. In addition, the ventriloquial voice is both the guarantee and the threat to the modern subject, who must learn to internalise power, as the subject gives itself the law through the medium of the voice, of the system, of self-speaking, and of self-overhearing, which Jacques Derrida has named 's'entendre parler'. In the light of these views, understanding the relation between the author and his/her voice becomes even more difficult. However, in any case, it is certain that the fictional character's writing or voice makes everything, (including the existence of an adult author, the character in the text, and the reader of the texts who receives such writing) variable, vague and of an uncertain *position*, so that, in the end, it allows these texts much potential.

As discussed thus far, the pattern of characters who write has various functions including, for example: generating plausibility and realism as a literary technique; representing subjectivity; agency and self-identity, as well as self-reflection of the writing persona; giving multiple perspectives; suggesting questions to readers. These numerous possibilities of understanding the texts with this pattern describe readers adequately, as well as writers of the texts, and, ultimately, the society and world where both belong. In particular, the recent spread of this pattern shows accurately the conditions and changes in our world society. A number of variations of subjectivity and self-identities, which are suggested by these texts, indicate the tolerance and acceptance required in society today, towards people who are different, from minorities, and perhaps deviant in a conventional sense. It also shows a great development in the use of perspectives in comparison with the situation in the past. According to John Stephens it used to be that a number of 'writers and authorities in the field of children's fiction have had a stake in promoting [a mode of reading which locates the reader only within the text] as a defence against what they perceive as the cultural threat of modernism' (1992: 4-5). Following this, it is possible to say that the increase in texts with a pattern including characters who write, indicates the coming of late modernity in the field of children's literature. According to Anthony Giddens, in this present-day world of what we call late modernity, 'the self, like the broader institutional contexts in which it exists, has to be reflexively made' (1991: 3), and in this respect, the increase of the motif of creating self, subjectivity and identity with their writing, proves the diversity of this society, as this pattern seems to be clearly suitable, or at least regarded to be so, in present-day society. As argued before, the image of a child writer can be interpreted negatively as a manipulated figure under adults' control. However, the multiplicity generated by this pattern, including all the possibilities discussed here, describes its openness and outlook, and, simultaneously, those of the world we live in. The world of books and our world are constantly influencing and representing each other.

Bibliography

Abbott, H. Porter (1984) *Diary Fiction: Writing as Action.* New York: Cornell University Press

Almond, David (1999) *Kit's Wilderness.* London: Hodder Children's Books

Anderson, Linda (2001) *Autobiography.* London: Routledge

Appleyard, J. A. (1991) *Becoming A Reader.* Cambridge: Cambridge University Press

Barthes, Roland (1987) 'The Death of the Author' in *Image, Music, Text,* Stephen Heath (ed.). London: Fontana, pp142-148

Chambers, Aidan (1982) *Dance On My Grave.* London: Red Fox

Chambers, Aidan (1990) 'The Reader in the Book' in *Children's Literature: The Development of Criticism,* Peter Hunt (ed.). London: Routledge, pp91-114

Chandler, Marilyn. R. (1990) *A Healing Art: Regeneration Through Autobiography.* New York & London: Garland Publishing

Cleary, Beverly (1983) *Dear Mr. Henshaw.* London: Julian MacRae Books

Connor, Steven (2000) *Dumbstruck: A Cultural History of Ventriloquism.* Oxford: Oxford University Press

Connor, Steven 'Steven Conner's Home Page'
[Available at http://www.bbk.ac.uk/eh/eng/staff/skcvent.htm]
(accessed 29/04/03)

Creech, Sharon (2001) *Love That Dog.* London: Bloomsbury

Doherty, Berlie (1991) *Dear Nobody.* London: Lions Tracks

Fitzhugh, Louise (1985) *Harriet the Spy.* First published 1964. London: Macmillan Education

Giddens, Anthony (1991) *Modernity and Self-Identity: Self and Society in the Late Modern Age.* Cambridge: Polity Press

McCallum, Robyn (1996) 'Metafictions and Experimental Work' in *The International Companion Encyclopaedia of Children's Literature*, Peter Hunt (ed.). London: Routledge, pp397-409

McCallum, Robyn (1999) *Ideologies of Identity in Adolescent Fiction.* London: Garland Publishing

McMaster, Juliet (2001) ''Adults' Literature,' By Children' in *The Lion and the Unicorn,* 25, 2, April, pp277-299

McNay, Lois (2000) *Gender and Agency: Reconfiguring the Subject in Feminist and Social Theory.* Cambridge: Polity Press

Marcus, Laura (1994) *Auto/biographical Discourses: Theory, Criticism, Practice.* Manchester: Manchester University Press

Mark, Jan (1991) *The Hillingdon Fox.* Stroud: Turton & Chambers Ltd.

Nikolajeva, Maria (1996) *Children's Literature Comes of Age: Toward a New Aesthetic.* London: Garland

Nikolajeva, Maria (2002) *The Rhetoric of Character in Children's Literature.* London: Scarecrow, pp223-267

O'Brien, Robert (1987) *Z for Zachariah.* London: Puffin

Rees, Celia (2000) *Witch Child* London: Bloomsbury

Ricœur, Paul (1985) *Time and Narrative.* Chicago and London: University of Chicago Press

Salinger, J. D. (1994) *The Catcher in the Rye.* First published in 1945. London: Penguin

Schwenke Wyile, Andrea (1999) 'Expanding the View of First-Person Narration' in *Children's Literature in Education,* 30, 3, pp185-202

Stephens, John (1992) *Language and Ideology in Children's Fiction.* London: Longman

Stephens, John (2002) 'A Page Just Waiting to Be Written On' in *Ways of Being Male: Representing Masculinities in Children's Literature and Film*, John Stephens (ed.). London: Routledge, pp38-54

Tashjian, Janet (2001) *The Gospel According to Larry.* New York: Henry Holt

Van Lieshout, Ted (2001) *Brothers.* London: HarperCollins

Wall, Barbara (1991) *The Narrator's Voice: The Dilemma of Children's Fiction.* London: Macmillan

Wilson, Jacqueline (1991) *The Story of Tracy Beaker.* London: Corgi Yearling Books

Is Holden Caulfield Still Real? The Body of Theory and Practice in Young Adult Literature

Alison Waller

> For years, the realms of 'theory' and 'fiction' have extended upon each other a strong attractive force, and nowhere more plainly than in the academic study of imaginative literature.
> (Bowie, 1987: 5)

> As a representation of a sixteen-year-old youth, the portrait of Holden achieves a timeless quality that is at variance with the novel's true status as a period piece.
> (Bloom, 1990: 1)

Harold Bloom's observation finds illustration in the literary comparisons, cultural allusions and passing references to J. D. Salinger's 'timeless' hero, which abound in various discourses of adolescence. Holden Caulfield is portrayed as the archetypal teenager, just as *The Catcher in the Rye* (1957) is often considered to be an archetypal teenage novel; yet both these assumptions are, to some extent, inaccurate. I would argue that popular assumptions about the figure of Holden Caulfield are symptomatic of a wider tendency within the discursive field of adolescence, to unquestioningly conflate fact and fiction, theory and representation.

This essay traces the discursive sphere in which Holden Caulfield functions, both as a universalised image of the teenager, and as a literary forbear for young adult fiction. This specific example serves to introduce broader issues of how fictional constructs are intimately bound to factual and theoretical discourses of adolescence. Edward Said's concepts of representation can usefully be employed to suggest that adolescence is not '*essentially* an idea, or a creation with no corresponding reality' but that it is 'a created body of theory and practice' in which fictional realisations play a major part (1978: 5). Like Orientalism, this process is politicised, as any discursive practice not only constructs knowledge but also controls it. In terms of young adult literature and the teenager, guiding impulses are usually moral and pedagogic, so that in defining adolescence, we also seek to shape and contain it. Here, then, I draw on previous 'constructivist' work in children's literature and propose a critical approach to teenage fiction which allows greater attentiveness to – and acceptance of – the shared meanings of fiction and theory. Although my reflections concentrate on young adults and their literature, they are also relevant to the broader field of children's literature.

Some early reviewers of *The Catcher in the Rye* showed concern over the effect that unsavoury content and coarse language might have on young readers, and in doing so revealed their belief that a book about a sixteen-year-old character is most likely to be read by sixteen-year-olds. Yet Salinger's novel was not originally published as a young adult text, partly because such a thing hardly existed until publishing houses created teenage imprints to cater for the youth market in the late 1960s. It is true that it has since been appropriated by teenage readers and placed on school curricula: but it is just as often enthusiastically adopted by an adult audience of scholars, critics and general readers. *Catcher* is then, in many ways, simultaneously an adult, and a young adult, novel. Much in the same way that Lewis Carroll's Alice resides in that uneasy location between adult curiosity and children's heroine, so Holden Caulfield has been considered suitable for both distanced adult amusement and the adolescent's eager identification (Bloom, 1990: 5-39).

If Caulfield is torn between two audiences he also exists in a perplexing position between fiction, fact and theory. In his most popular guise outside of the novel, he acts as a reference for the literary or film review. Recent appearances include the following: Russell Banks' *Rule of the Bone* (1995) is described as '*The Catcher in the Rye* for the nineties' due to similarities between the main characters; Vernon, in D. B. C. Pierre's *Vernon God Little* (2003) is 'a millennial Holden Caulfield, a child of Jerry Springer and Eminem'; the film *Igby Goes Down* (Steers: 2002) is hardly ever reviewed without comparisons being made between Igby and Caulfield. Moreover, in discussing young adult novels and the possibility (or impossibility) of identifying 'real adolescence', Karín Lesnik-Oberstein argues that Holden Caulfield has 'an iron grip' on young adult literature and its criticism. By this she means that his brand of adolescence – as 'questioning, and seeing through, the hypocrisy and corruption of the adult world' – influences other fictional characters *and* the way that critics read them (1998: 25).

But Caulfield is not merely a literary trope to be rediscovered in contemporary fiction. He also functions as a character model that can be applied in much wider contexts: to describe public figures, for example. George Bush and John MacEnroe are amongst an eclectic group of individuals to be referred to as Holden Caulfield types and, despite obvious diversities, the reference to Caulfield aims to self-evidently and unproblematically unite them.

It is clear that although Caulfield is a fictive character, his significance extends beyond literature and literary representations. It reaches as far as those discourses which claim direct access to reality or empirical knowledge: the sciences of adolescence – particularly psychology. David Elkind's 1967 essay on egocentricism, for example, illustrates certain dialogic tendencies that emerge in theorising adolescence. One feature of Elkind's concept of egocentricism is the 'personal fable', which refers to the image an adolescent creates of themselves as a unique and special person. In describing this, he writes that 'the emotional torments undergone by Salinger's Holden Caulfield exemplify the adolescent's belief in the uniqueness of his own emotional experience' (p93). The familiar process of using fictional representations to support an empirical finding is here rendered unclear. Does Elkind mean that reading and identifying with the story of Caulfield provides us with evidence of the adolescent's personal fable, or does Caulfield's existence itself (albeit fictional) prove the validity of Elkind's concept because he fits the model?

Certainly Elkind seems to be claiming a kind of validity and typicality in the character of Caulfield who, by the time Elkind was writing his theory in the 1960s, had reached archetypal status. Yet, as I indicated above, Salinger's hero is neither real nor conventional. As a fictional representation of a sixteen-year-old he may offer some authentic characteristics, but it seems problematic to base any aspect of a theory of normal adolescence on a character who is possibly neurotic, periodically in therapy, and always a dramatic, fictional construct. (The predicament becomes more sinister when we consider that Mark Chapman assassinated John Lennon under the banner of Caulfield and his distaste for anything phony). Moreover, in *Catcher*, Caulfield inhabits 1950s Manhattan, and some of the narrative tension arises from his dissatisfaction with New York as a legitimate place for adolescent experience. The concept of the teenager as a social group with separate needs was emergent at this point in America, and Caulfield is partly shaped by the fact that he cannot be absorbed into a youth culture because it does not yet fully exist. This context is ignored by Elkind who writes just ten years later: and it is ignored by any contemporary critic who refers to Caulfield as a universal figure of adolescence, writing in a new century when the teenager arguably has a more central role in culture and society.

Extricating ourselves from Holden Caulfield's iron grip, it is necessary to consider *why* this fictional character has proven to be so influential in literary and non-literary fields, and what this means for criticism. To do this, we can turn to a more general discussion of the adolescent in young adult literature. Lesnik-Oberstein, amongst other constructivist critics, has already crucially advanced debate about how criticism desires and constructs a 'real child' in order to validate texts and their readings. She complains that criticism of teenage fiction rarely 'questions, deconstructs, or 'destabilizes' 'adolescence' as the central 'real' identity and perspective, either within the novels, or outside the novels' (1998: 25). In other words, critics still do not generally engage with Jacqueline Rose's 'child behind the category 'children's literature'' (1984: 10) in order to understand their own ideological stance towards this literature. Lesnik-Oberstein coherently sets out the perimeters of this constructed child, or adolescent, and is clear about the ways in which children's literature criticism draws upon scientific models and fictional representations. However, much less emphasis is placed on how this process is complicated by a flow of representations from theory to fiction or fiction to theory. Said (1978) describes the traffic between academic and imaginative representations of the Orient, and a similar methodology can help to re-read teenage fiction through the roles that theory and fiction play in constructing adolescence. I will return later to Lesnik-Oberstein's anxiety about young adult and children's literature criticism.

In one of the quotations cited at the opening of this essay, Bowie argues that theory and fiction have an integral connection, and that this exists 'nowhere more plainly than in the academic study of imaginative literature.' (1987: 5) Perhaps it is worth adding that this force exists nowhere more plainly than in the study of young adult literature. This is not only because criticism of teenage fiction has traditionally been unwilling to avoid judgements about the relevance, appropriateness, or authenticity of these novels for adolescence and adolescent readers, measuring the narratives against social, psychological and educational theories or demands. It is also due to the nature of teenage fiction itself, which finds itself intertwined with ethical and pedagogical issues.

Young adult literature exists within a matrix of discourses of the adolescent, and is necessarily affected by its position in relation to social theory, educational policy and developments in psychological and biological knowledge. Over the relatively short history of the study of adolescence (originating with Granville Stanley Hall's 1904 volumes on the subject) the dominant approach has been broadly humanist: defining and understanding in order to encourage positive and normal individuals. During the 1970s and 80s, for example, much sociological research on youth focused on the social problems created by deviant or delinquent teenagers, often through the agency of popular culture, music, film and fashion (Griffin, 1993: 131-157, 203). Literature written and published in this critical atmosphere found itself attacked for teaching the wrong messages: Judy Blume's *Forever* (1975) invoked fears of encouraging teenage sexual experiences through its description of Katherine's exceptionally cautious sexual relationship with Michael. Melvin Burgess's *Doing It* ((2003) continues the debate over 25 years later, reflecting more explicit sexual knowledge available to young people. Conversely, by dealing with a subject that social or psychological theory has specified as crucial to adolescence – or that mass media has highlighted as a key theme of youth culture – other novels have been welcomed as a positive influence on a problem sector of society. Either way, the commercial success of young adult literature often relies on the educational context in which even reluctant (male) readers have to consume. Reading lists, library shelves and school curricula for the teenager are not independent of wider understandings of what this teenager is and what they should be.

Moreover, Peter Hunt demands that children's and teenage fiction is 'of the moment'. According to him, part of the definition of this fiction must be 'that a particular text was written expressly for children who are recognizably children, with a childhood recognizable today' (1996: 16); and this may offer further enlightenment about the interplay between fiction and theory. A form of writing written expressly for recognisable teenagers is, in some respects, a circular concept because although early Young Adult fiction was created in response to a teenage market, it was also partly responsible for shaping that very phenomenon. For if Georg Lukác's claim is correct, that art is a form of knowledge that shares the same goal as science in aiming to show things as they really are, it can be argued that teenage realism emerged at the same time as many scientific theories of adolescence, because authors and theorists both needed to represent a newly conceived and increasingly important section of society.

This recognisable adolescence, then, is found in moral and educational impulses, in commercial drives, and in the fictions expressly presented to young readers in young adult literature. There is also, of course, a tangible thread running from fiction and theory to individuals who live the content of social models and read the teenage novels. How is it possible to relate the individual teenager to the web of fact and fiction that we have discovered, without feeling the need to speak to every reader or caveat every generalisation with a specific illustration? A useful approach is taken up by Stephen Thomson in his discussion of Melvin Burgess's *Junk*, returning to the crucial issue of teenage identity as 'of the moment':

> while, on the one hand, the specific paraphernalia of a youth phenomenon such as punk are the very essence of the experience of being young at a certain time, they are also, *sub specie aeternitatis*, dispensable, extrinsic, just one possible décor draped over an abiding and essentially unchanging scene of youth as such. (1999: 23-24)

The suggestion is that adolescence is the performance of a role, a draping of one of the possible decors offered amongst diverse discourses of youth. As a performer, the teenager is free to take on any of the roles on offer but also to remain distinct from any of them: not to be the sum of their parts. Indeed, this corresponds to Said's assertion that identities are bodies of theory *and practice* (1978). Performance is also a strong theme in many of the specific discourses of the teenager: whether that is Elkind's 'personal fable' (and 'imaginary audience'); the social theories of youth where performative subcultures act as 'magical' solutions to cultural conflict (Brake, 1980: 1-25); or in literary criticism of the archetypal Caulfield. Thomson claims that the roles offered to adolescents are often playfully appropriated, 'not least because the greater part of the roles on offer are judged, in the language of Holden Caulfield, phony' (Thomson, 1999: 23).

The discussion above has explored the ways that factual and fictional boundaries refuse to remain discrete in the discursive field of adolescence. As illustration we have seen how the figure of Holden Caulfield cuts through all kinds of processes for constructing adolescence, from literary versions of youth to theoretical models and common-sense meanings. But how can this understanding enrich current research in teenage (and children's) literature? It is already recognised that children's literature acts to create and control images of childhood in a wider context, and this theoretical understanding can usefully be extended to teenage fiction criticism. Indeed, it might be argued that the teenager is more explicitly constructed as a recent cultural and social category and that fictions have a greater share in the discourse of adolescence. Rose, Lesnik-Oberstein, and other constructivist critics express anxiety about the conflating of fact and fiction in children's literature but I would suggest that this conflation is not only inevitable but also valuable. The fruitful criticism generated by deconstructing ideas of the real teenager and the real teenage reader might be enhanced by an acceptance of the virtues of traffic between academic and imaginative representations.

In acknowledging fluidity between the real and the constructed we can return to Holden Caulfield. It is evident that in this essay there has not been space to discuss the historical, geographical, racial or gendered implications of Caulfield's significance: that he is an American adolescent and one created at a time when youth culture exploded in the States is clearly important due to the dominance of American models of adolescence, and issues of nostalgia and excitement surrounding the emergence of the teenager in the 1950s. That he is male and white may say more about desires to construct an archetype through the traditionally dominant markers of identity in Western society. Which figure from more recent, British culture might claim a similar agency in discourses of adolescence? The answers are, at present, necessarily speculative. Perhaps the image of the British teenager is less glamorous and more a figure of derision or irony – an idea supported by the fact that the comic creation Kevin the Teenager functions as archetype in much the same way as Holden Caulfield does, but to suggest a sense of pathetic teen sullenness rather than glamorous adolescent angst. Or else Harry Potter is the emergent adolescent paradigm, in which case children's and young adult literature criticism has a stimulating task ahead in examining the creative exchange between fictional representations, empirical exposition, cultural theory and the development of fantasies and narratives for young people.

Bibliography

Banks, Russell (1995) *Rule of the Bone.* London: Secker & Warburg

Bloom, Harold (1990) *Holden Caulfield.* New York: Chelsea House Publishers

Blume, Judy (1975) *Forever.* London: Victor Gollancz

Bowie, Malcolm (1987) *Freud, Proust and Lacan: Theory as Fiction.* Cambridge: Cambridge University Press

Brake, Mike (1980) *The Sociology of Youth Culture and Youth Subcultures: Sex and Drugs and Rock'n'roll?* London: Routledge

Burgess, Melvin (1996) *Junk.* London: Anderson Press

Burgess, Melvin (2003) *Doing It.* London: Anderson Press

Elkind, David (1981) 'Egocentricism in Adolescents' in *Children and Adolescents: Interpretive Essays on Jean Piaget*, David Elkind (ed.). Oxford: Oxford University Press, pp74-95

Griffin, Christine (1993) *Representations of Youth: the Study of Youth and Adolescence in Britain and America.* Cambridge: Polity Press

Hall, Granville Stanley (1904) *Adolescence: Its Psychology and its Relation to Physiology, Anthropology, Sociology, Sex, Crime, Religion, and Education.* New York: D. Appleton & Co.

Hunt, Peter (1996) 'Defining Children's Literature' in *Only Connect*, 3rd ed., Sheila Egoff, et al. (eds.). Oxford: Oxford University Press, pp2-17

Lesnik-Oberstein, Karín (1994) *Children's Literature: Criticism and the Fictional Child.* Oxford: Oxford University Press

Lesnik-Oberstein, Karín (ed.) (1998) *Children in Culture: Approaches to Childhood.* London: Macmillan

Lukác, Georg (1970) *Writer and Critic.* London: Merlin Press

Pierre, D. B. C. (2003) *Vernon God Little.* London: Faber & Faber

Rose, Jacqueline (1984) *The Case of Peter Pan, or the Impossibility of Children's Fiction.* London: Macmillan

Said, Edward (1978) *Orientalism.* London: Penguin

Salinger, J. D. (1951) *The Catcher in the Rye.* London: Penguin

Steers, Burr (2002) *Igby Goes Down*. U.S.A.: United Artists & Atlantic Streamline

Thomson, Stephen (1999) 'The Real Adolescent: Performance and Negativity in Melvyn Burgess's *Junk*' in *The Lion & the Unicorn,* 23, 1, January, pp22-29

Proposing a Methodology for the Study of Nation(ality) in Children's Literature

Dominique Sandis

In an age of globalisation, with political and cultural borders constantly being merged and lost, a strong general concern regarding nation and national identity (for reasons of brevity the term nation(ality) shall be used throughout the essay encompassing the notions of nation, culture, national character and identity) has become apparent in discourse surrounding children's literature.[1] The presence of nation, national character and culture as well as stereotype and the image of the other in this literature not only hold interest on a literary (see Lucas, 1997; McCallum, 1997; Meek, 2001; and Webb, 2000) level but also on a social and educational one due to the properties of socialisation which this literature is seen to hold: '[n]o images in literature are more compelling than those found in literature for children as they formulate how children come to see and understand the world' (Austin & Whatley, 2001: 3).

Albeit the developing critical interest in the literary manifestations of nation(ality), it is surprising that no truly adequate general methodology for the study of its literary construction has been tendered. This has not gone unnoticed in children's literature research whereupon Nikolajeva has stated that despite the significant number of studies into nation(ality) 'so far no satisfactory analytical tools or general theory has been proposed'. (1999: 10) Previous studies into the image of nation(ality) in children's literature have been divided by O'Sullivan (1990: 26-27) into four categories:

- 'theme and motif' studies categorising and cataloguing the occurrence of one nation (or more) in the literature of another (i.e. the image of the native or the African American in multicultural American picture books, etc.); (Dowd, 1992; Ipsiroglu, 1996; Monroe, 1997; Rutschmann, 2000);

- studies categorising and cataloguing, however not as an end in themselves, i.e. to ascertain the influence of biography in the image of the foreigner, or the influence of politics and history in the image, comparison of image of 'self' between national literatures to determine historical influence on social self-image, etc. Neo Historicism or Postcolonial theory often contributes to the theoretical and methodological frameworks; (Hancock, 1997; Little, 1998; O'Sullivan, 2000; Anagnostopoulou, 2002; Bainbridge, 2001; Thistleton-Martin, 2002);

- studies which trace the history and genesis of specific stereotypes and ultimately encompass theoretical contributions on the general development and dissemination of notions of other people in and through literature; (O'Sullivan 1990; Yenika-Agbaw, 1990);

- and imagological studies (O'Sullivan 1990 and 1995; Perrot, 1998; Fellman, 2003).

A fifth category can be added to the above, namely that of studies tracing the history, categorising, and cataloguing the national identity of the 'home nation' in its national literature (Diakiw, 1996 &1997; Bainbridge & Wolodko, 2001; Kanatsouli, 2002; Williams, 2003).

Studies which have made use of the theoretical and methodological framework of imagology, a specialisation of comparative literature focusing on the 'discursive and literary articulation of cultural difference and of national identity' (Leerssen, 2000: 268-9), have provided the most adequate methodologies in the literary construction of nation(ality). In particular, and drawing from the methodology of imagological studies in both adult and children's literature (Pageaux, 1989; O'Sullivan, 1990; Leerssen, 2000), it is important to investigate and evaluate, in their literary contexts, 'a multitude of factors influencing how one nation is seen and portrayed by another at any specific point in history' (O'Sullivan, 1990: 27). Imagology further stresses the significance of contrast by emphasising the bi-polarity of the elements under analysis (i.e. north geographic location of author versus south location of constructed nation; strong versus weak, etc.) as well as that of the hetero- and auto-self. Finally, imagology does not concern itself with 'reality' but only with the literary construction and its components. Since common denominators or distinguishing features of a nation and national literature can be revealed only through contrast with literature of other countries or regions (Spiering, 1992; Nikolajeva, 1999; Fox, 2001), the source of a satisfactory methodology for the literary study of nation(ality) would logically be found within the framework of comparative literature.

Taking the latter into consideration, one might assume that studies into nation(ality) would have been able to draw indiscriminately from the methodology of imagology, however, as with its 'maternal' theory comparative literature, the methodology of this theory is fragmented and in a state of desideratum (Economou-Agorastou, 1992). This is self-explanatory if one reads descriptions of comparative literary methodology ranging from Siaflekis' 'comparison' (1984) to Prawer's slightly more specific 'comparison across linguistic barriers' (1973), to others' 'comparison across national borders or across cultures' (Politou-Marmarinou, 1981; Bassnett, 1993).

Comparatist Totosy de Zepetnek has highlighted this problem and has questioned whether this may be the reason for which:

comparative literature, either as the translation of literatures and cultures (as in a conceptual and ideological translation and/or as an actual translation) or as a cross-cultural inclusionary ideology and practice is assumed to be a methodology per se (1999: 3).

It is hard to imagine that the above-described studies (which have made use of a number of different literary but also other disciplinary theories) have not been able to propose a 'satisfactory' methodology for the analysis of nation(ality) in children's literature. The main problem, however, is not that the methodologies are not of value in each particular case, but rather that none of them have been able to succeed in proposing a clear and universally applicable methodology for the study of the literary construction of the subject. Furthermore, in many instances, the methodologies have been just as abstract as the notions encompassed by the term nation(ality) itself. A satisfactory methodology for such a difficult theme should be clear, solid and practical. To illustrate, here are a few general problems encountered:

- Although images of nations are usually described, categorised and then interpreted through the use of valid theoretical frameworks, their literary construction and components are rarely focussed upon.

- Although it is valuable that main theoretical frameworks such as those of new historicism and postcolonialism are used, such frameworks have involved interpretations and reasoning for the images presented in the literature. These interpretations, valuable on a sociological basis, do not have much to offer on a literary level due to the problem related to reality, the ambiguity of the author, ideologies at work, etc.

- It is common for the images to be examined and interpreted in terms of their accuracy to reality (stereotype/multicultural evaluation/image of the other, etc.). This aspect of reality and accuracy is one which is ambiguous and brings forward a series of questions which make such interpretations problematic.

- Although the function of stereotype, its development and dissemination, has been studied meticulously, its literary elements and construction has been mainly ignored. In addition, the focus on stereotype presupposes knowledge of reality or 'kernel of truth' (Allport in O'Sullivan, 1990: 20). This presupposition thus brings doubt on studies that maintain they have no interest in the aspect of reality. In studying the literary construction of nation(ality), the researcher is not interested in the realism of the construction but in the manner and components of that construction.

- The methodologies have not always been clear as to how the particular identities and images were distinguished in the primary texts, i.e. through questionnaires, through close reading, etc.

- Most studies have been mainly involved in determining and presenting the image of the other in literature or of the 'self' in the home national literature, however these images have not been compared to each other, i.e. the construction of the image of the 'self' by the 'other' compared to that of the image of the 'self' by the home culture (in literature).

Nikolajeva's (1999) emphatic statement in addition to the methodological 'gaps' mentioned above, has instigated a working hypothesis whereby a satisfactory methodological tool or model for the study of the literary construct of nation(ality) may be tendered if we draw from the theories of comparative literature, (especially imagology and translation theories), intertextuality and cultural studies. Such an interdisciplinary methodology seems to be the most comprehensive manner in which to approach this both abstract and subjective notion comprised of so many different elements of the human mindscape. And it is through the distinction and ultimate analysis of these particular elements that the literary construct of nation(ality) can be studied.

The defining components of nation designate a form of living, a recipe for social living whether this be in the society of a 'primitive to today's Western World' tribe or in that of a modern city (or, as Eagleton describes it, 'the culture of Bavaria or Microsoft or the Bushmen' (2000: 20)). Upon their transfer to a fictional milieu, political and cultural elements, geographical and racial aspects, as well as ideologies and historical influences that make up nations in reality change considerably (Renan, 1990). These elements also include dimensions particular to literature such as intertextuality and narrative techniques. Furthermore, when a nation other than that of the author's nationality is constructed in literature the elements creating the 'other' nation encompass elements of the author's own nation and thus the new fictionally created 'other nation' becomes a combination of two nations. Language also becomes an important factor in the construction of literary nation(ality) as it is a vehicle of nation(ality) in itself (i.e. vocabulary particular to a nation, expressions, etc.). In literature, when the language of the constructed differs from that of the constructor, elements of identity encompassed in the language of the constructor infiltrate the literary nation(ality) of the 'other' (Lanehart, 1996).

Taking the above into consideration, and in difference to prior studies (other than imagology) the elements composing nation(ality) shall be drawn from the literature itself and not from 'reality'. Due to the subjective and personal nature of nation(ality), finding the components or indicators of identity in the 'real world' proves not only complex and difficult as a method (i.e. the Katz and Braly paradigm in Brigham), unreliable in regard to the results ('in most cases, no criteria are available for assessing the factual validity of an ethnic generalisation' (Brigham, 1971: 17)), but also unnecessary in this particular methodology. Such results, other than in the case of interests of accuracy of literary constructions to 'reality', would not prove useful, as 'we have become accustomed to viewing our representational activity in terms, not of 'fidelity to empirical reality', but of 'recognisability' in a set of conventions' (Leerssen, 1991: 165). These conventions, constituting our framework of understanding the notion of nation(ality), are present in national literature and once distinguished, may be categorised as components and assembled in the form of a methodological model.

National literature has been described as 'narratives produced by a culture [that] are models by which a society conceives of and articulates a view of itself' (Turner in McCallum, 1997: 101) and which have 'traditionally been seen as a reflection of the values, tensions, myths and psychology that identify a national character' (Bainbridge & Thistleton-Martin). It is a literature in which national, moral and political concerns both past and present are embedded whether consciously or unconsciously. As it has become increasingly difficult to distinguish national literature due to the influx of multicultural, transcultural, and diasporic literatures, national children's literature may be defined as the literature produced in a certain country by a national of that country (whether a member of a minority or a second generation and later immigrant), written in the language of the country (minority, however not immigrant, languages included) and whereupon the plot is in its majority set in that country.

The results of a number of studies concerned with the 'home-identity' in national literature which have identified elements of nation(ality), have proved significant in the formulation of the methodological model. In a study of multiculturalism and Hellenicity, Greek children's literature scholar Kanatsouli (2002) identified elements of Hellenic nation and identity as they appeared in the Hellenic national literature. These were categorised under the following general headings; customs and traditions, religion, history, cultural heritage, mythological references, and geographical particularities. They were further exemplified with the listing of sub-elements under each main category. Working on the same motif, Bainbridge and Wolodko (2001) examined Canadian children's literature at the beginning of the twenty-first century in order to ascertain what commonplaces of Canadian culture and identity identified in earlier research by Diakiw (1996) were present. In conclusion to their research, Bainbridge and Wolodko determined that just as Diakiw 'makes the point that the layering of the ten commonplaces produces a distinctive Canadian culture, it is this same layering that is reflected in Canadian books for children, and it is that which makes them unique and utterly Canadian.' (1996: 59) Stephens, in a previous paper, also identified the most common images of Australian society in Australian children's literature. What is interesting about these studies is that they distinguish similar or identical commonplaces as components of nation in their national literatures. This should not be at all strange if one is to accept social anthropologist Lévi-Strauss's postulation 'that all cultures are formed of the same basic elements, just as all sentences are formed of the same basic parts of speech' (Nodelman, 1996: 181).

Drawing from the results of the above studies, the elements distinguished are then checked against two cultural paradigms presented by Pratt and Beaty (1999) and Jobe (1993) in studies concerned with multicultural and transcultural literature and their potential in education for the promotion of international understanding. In these paradigms, the main elements making up culture have been identified. The elements are almost identical to those found in the national literature. Pratt and Beaty's model includes the following elements: geographic location, economic system, political system and social system. These categories are further divided into smaller units. Pratt and Beaty illustrate how:

> all societies seem to contain these four elements ... the detailed nature of one society may differ markedly from that of another even though the four elements appear to be very similar in each. Similarly, even though all four elements are comparable in two or more societies, their complex interplay can yield distinct cultural differences. (p7)

Jobe's paradigm is different from that of Pratt and Beaty because, although he distinguishes the elements that make up culture, he also distinguishes the visual and language markers of culture. These markers are closer to the methodological model to be proposed in this paper for they are drawn from the cultural constructions in literature. Jobe's (pp24-25) visual and implied indicators are the following: personal (i.e. dress, costume, jewellery, food, artefacts, tools, and activities); setting (i.e. landscapes, famous landmarks, and buildings, houses, markets); cultural indicators (i.e. colour; design, patterns, objects, places, and characters); and cultural attitudes (i.e. posture, position, values, respect, social conventions, generational indicators and gender indicators). Jobe further distinguishes language and narrative indicators which are of utmost importance in the construction of nation and culture in literature: language patterns (including names, specific expressions, dialogue and storytelling patterns) and narrative patterns (including traditional opening phrase, story type, story structure, and traditional conclusion). At this point the main elements of the model have been obtained, however there are still two further steps which have to be taken to assure that all indices have been checked.

In agreement with Kuran-Burcoglu (2000), who has pinpointed the potential intersecting spheres of translation studies and imagology and highlighted the possibility of developing research in both disciplines in an interdisciplinary manner, the model draws from Translation Studies. Carus has also stated that 'there is no better way to find out about the national character of any country than to search for the untranslatable words in its language.' (1980: 177) This can be said in reference to ideas that are particular to a nation or identity. Nikolajeva terms the notion that Carus describes as the 'zone of non-translatability' (1996: 29) and distinguishes the following main elements: i) everyday life (i.e. everyday objects, food, clothes, routines); ii) human relations, (i.e. communication and behaviour rituals); and iii) the linguistic level of the semiosphere (i.e. colloquialisms, dialect, babytalk and four letter words). Klingberg (1986), in his seminal work on children's literature in translation, has also worked dynamically in this area of 'non-translatability' and has compiled a list of specific problems in the translation of children's literature. The main problems are those caused by elements of nation specific to the source text and which cannot be easily translated into the language of the target text or, even in the same language for a different cultural audience (i.e. in the domestication of the Harry Potter books for North American audiences). Klingberg distinguishes that elements such as literary references, references to mythology and popular belief, historical, religious and political background, buildings and home furnishings, food, customs and practices, flora and fauna, personal and geographical names, are the most troublesome. These elements of 'non-translatability', checked against those obtained from the national literature and those from the cultural paradigms discussed above, are again the same primary elements that construct nation and national identity in literature.

The final point that has to be considered in order to complete the formulation of the methodological model is that of intertextuality. 'The text is a tissue of quotations drawn from the innumerable centres of culture ... [the author's] only power is to mix writings, to counter the ones with the others, in such a way as never to rest on any one of them ...' (Barthes in Bassnett, 1998: 27). Although usually used to illustrate Barthes's 'The Death of the Author', in this case this quotation is useful in the illustration of the text as a creation of culture and nation. A combination of different cultural elements, the text also includes references to other texts (usually of the national literature canon), commonplace objects, names, media, etc. Intertextuality is not only

considered, in translation theory, as an element in the area of 'non-translatability', but it is also considered a 'cultural obstacle' in cases in which texts are used in their original language in foreign language classes (Rönnqvist, 2002). The intertextual elements distinguished are clearly a direct reference to national identity. A clear example of this is the weaving of popular or folk-tales and canonical national literature into the plot. Even if most of the components of nation(ality) are used less in a text, intertextuality on its own can adequately transfer all notions of nation.
The general components used for the literary construction of nation(ality) and which indicate nation(ality) in literary texts, are the following:

Customs and Tradition
Religion
History and Cultural Heritage
Language and Linguistic Particularities
Geography / Flora and Fauna
Society / Everyday Life and Objects
Ideology / Politics
Narrative Particularities
Intertextuality

They have been distinguished in national literatures, checked against literary cultural paradigms, and then against the 'area of non-translatability' proposed in translation studies. In addition to the conventional indication of nation(ality), these components further encompass aspects specific to literature such as intertextuality and narrative particularities.

But how can this model be used as or within a methodology? An example could be its use in the form of a questionnaire to be completed during the close reading of texts being analysed whereupon the particular elements are searched for during the reading. In most cases, it is possible to find, through the use of this model, the nation(ality) and the components used for its construction in any literature being studied. A further use of this model would be to question the elements used in the construction of the 'self' (i.e. Greek national identity) in the home literature (Greek children's literature) to the construction of the 'other' (Greek national identity) in foreign literature (English-language literature, or French national literature). Such a study would distinguish, for example, which of the above elements are used more when the nation(ality) is constructed by the 'self' or by the 'other'. On the other, if only the 'self' is being studied, the use of this model could be used, in the study of children's literature of a particular time period, to distinguish what the most important elements of construction of identity are and if, for example the literature of the nineteenth century in comparison to that of the twentieth century uses more elements of religion, history and ideology rather than linguistic and narrative particularities. Such results could be used in the discussion of globalisation and multiculturalism whereupon national identity is more subtly and indirectly emphasised than in the previous century. A further use of this model could be to distinguish the components of the model in a particular text and then compare the results to those found in a translation of the text. In this way it can be ascertained which particular components are most changed upon their transfer to another language, i.e. which components undergo most domestication or foreignisation. This model of components of nation(ality) can also be used to check and ascertain how national identity is constructed in multicultural, transcultural and diasporic literatures and how these constructions differ from the national literatures. The components of the model, however, do not need to be used together, and components can be studied in literature on their own. An example of this could be a study of narrative particularities (i.e. lyrical prose, fragmentation of prose, poetry, etc.) in a particular national literature, which is then compared to the narrative particularities of another national literature. Are the same particularities present in the construction of the nation(ality) by 'another'?

Having proposed the model above, it remains clear that it has not been illustrated as fully as possible albeit the few examples above and it certainly requires further development. However, as this paper, which is part of postgraduate work in progress dealing with the construction of Hellenic nation(ality) in English-language children's literature set during political and historical events in Modern Greece, it is intended that this model shall act as a beginning to the development of a general theory in the study of a subject that is becoming more and more prominent in literary studies. Finally, this paper has attempted to propose a methodological tool which, although it has its source in children's literature research, can ultimately be applied to adult literary research as well. Children's literature may seem to be a minor or peripheral literature in the great wide world of literature, but in truth, along with its thematology, its special nature due to its authorship and readership, and also its narrative techniques, it may serve, in literary research, as a fertile ground for the proposal of literary theory and methodology which can be applied not only to further research within itself but also within other literary fields and discourses. Nikolajeva has quoted Yuri Lotman as having said that 'in every system it is the boundary and the periphery that are the active zones' (1999: 25), thus it is from this active periphery of the world of children's literature that new ideas and methodologies in literary research can develop and grow. It is further especially important that a methodological framework for the study of nation and cultural be proposed within the context of children's literature since 'even more so than adult literature, children's literature evolves from international, rather than national, paradigms' (Bouckaert-Ghesquiere in O'Sullivan, 1996: 285). Bringing together national children's literatures through comparative literature research (a marriage between the 'Cinderella' subjects of the literary world) may ultimately allow for these two subjects to ultimately come out of the 'marginal literatures' category and into the mainstream academic literary world.

Bibliography

Anagnostopoulou, Diamanti (2002) 'Logotechnia ke Eterotita: I Ennia ke I Ikona tou Xenou ke tou Diaforetikou se Logotechnikes Afigiseis gia Pedia' presented at the 3rd Panhellenic Conference of the Department of Primary School Education of the Kapodistrian University of Athens entitled: Logotechnia Simera: Opseis, Anatheoriseis, December 2002

Austin, Patricia & Whatley, April (2001) 'From the Editors: Weaving the Strands of Images' in *Journal of Children's Literature,* 27, 2, Fall, p3-4

Bainbridge, Joyce, & Thistleton-Martin, Judy 'Children's Literature: Vehicle for the transmission of national culture and identity or the victim of mass market globalisation?'
[Available at: http://www.ualberta.ca/~jb5/homepage.htm#publications] (accessed 27/8/2002)

Bainbridge, Joyce & Wolodko, Brenda (2001) 'The 'Canadian' in Canadian Children's Literature' in *Journal of Children's Literature,* 27, 2, Fall, pp52-60

Bassnett, Susan (1993) *Comparative Literature: A Critical Introduction.* Oxford: Blackwell

Bassnett, Susan (1998) 'When Is A Translation Not A Translation' in *Constructing Cultures: Essays on Literary Translation*, Susan Bassnett, Andre Lefevre (eds.). Clarendon: Multilingual Matters, pp25-40

Brigham, John C. (1971) 'Ethnic Stereotypes' in *Psychological Bulletin,* 76, 1, July, pp15-38

Carus, Marianne (1980) 'Translation and Internationalism in Children's Literature' in *Children's Literature in Education,* 11, 4, pp171-179

Diakiw, Jerry (1996) 'The School's Role in Revealing the Commonplaces of our National Culture and Identity: A Multicultural Perspective' in *Multicultural Education: The State of the Art National Study, Report #4*, Keith McLeod (ed.). Winnipeg: Canadian Association of Second Language Teachers, pp26-39

Diakiw, Jerry (1997) 'Children's Literature and Canadian National Identity: A Revisionist Perspective' in *Canadian Children's Literature,* 87, 23, 3, Fall, pp36-49.

Dowd, Frances Smardo (1992) 'Evaluating Children's Books Portraying Native American and Asian Cultures' in *Childhood Education,* 68, 4, Summer, pp219-224

Eagleton, Terry (2000) *The Idea of Culture.* Oxford: Blackwell

Economou-Agorastou, Ioanna (1992) *Isagogi sti Singritiki Stereotipologia ton Ethnikon Charaktiristikon sti Logotechnia.* Thessaloniki: University Studio Press

Fellman, Elin (2003) 'From Image to Icon: The Cultural Metamorphosis of Illustrated Children's Books as Exemplified by Winnie-the-Pooh'. Project Description. Abo Akademi

Fox, Carol (2001) 'Conflicting Fictions: National Identity in English Children's Literature About War' in *Children's Literature and National Identity*, Margaret Meek (ed.). Stoke on Trent: Trentham Books, pp43-52

Hancock, Ian (1987) 'The Origin and Function of the Gypsy Image in Children's Literature' in *The Lion and the Unicorn,* 11, 1, pp47-59

Ipsiroglu, Zehra (1996) 'Türkeibilder in der Deutschen Kinder- und Jugendliteratur' in *Beiträge Jugendliteratur und Medien,* 48, 1, pp2-10

Jobe, Ronald A. (1993) *Cultural Connections: Using Literature to Explore World Cultures with Children.* Markham, Ontario: Pembroke

Kanatsouli, Meni (2002) *Amfisima tis Pedikis Logotechnias.* Athens: Sinchroni Orizontes

Klingberg, Göte (1986) *Children's Fiction in the Hands of Translators.* Malmö: CWK Gleerup

Kuran-Burçoglu, Nedret (2000) 'At the Crossroads of Translation Studies and Imagology' in *Translation in Context: Selected Contributions from the EST Congress, Granada 1998*, A. Chesterman, N. Gallardo San Salvador, Y. Gambier (eds.). Amsterdam: Rodopi, pp143-150

Lanehart, Sonja L. (1996) 'The Language of Identity' in *Journal of English Linguistics,* 24, 4, pp322-331

Leerssen, Joep. Th. (1991) 'Echoes and Images: Reflections upon Foreign Space' in *Alterity, Identity, Image: Selves and Others in Society and Scholarship*, Raymond Corbey, Joep Th. Leerssen (eds.). Amsterdam: Rodopi, pp123-138

Leerssen, Joep. Th. (2000) 'The Rhetoric of National Character: A Programmatic Survey' in *Poetics Today,* 21, 1, pp269-292

Little, Greta D. (1998) 'Vicarious Culture Shock: Children's Books about North Africa' in *Critical Perspectives on Postcolonial African Children's and Young Adult Literature*, Meena Khorana (ed.). London: Greenwood Press, pp87-100

Lucas, Ann Lawson (ed.) (1997) *Gunpowder and Sealing-Wax: Nationhood in Children's Literature.* Leicester: Troubador

McCallum, Robyn (1997) 'Cultural Solipsism, National Identities and the Discourse of Multiculturalism in Australian Picture Books' in *ARIEL: A Review of International English Literature,* 28, 1, January, pp101-116

Meek, Margaret (ed.) (2001) *Children's Literature and National Identity.* Stoke on Trent: Trentham Books

Monroe, Susanne S. (1997) 'Beyond Pocahontas: Authentic Images of Native American Females in Children's Literature' in *The New Advocate,* 10, 2, Spring, pp149-159

Nikolajeva, Maria (1996) *Children's Literature Comes of Age: Towards A New Aesthetic.* New York: Garland

Nikolajeva, Maria (1999) 'Similar but Separate: National Features in Scandinavian Children's Literature' in *Bookbird,* 37, 4, pp6-10

Nodelman, Perry (1996) *The Pleasures of Children's Literature.* 2nd edition. White Plains, New York: Longman

O'Sullivan, Emer (1990*) Friend and Foe: The Image of Germany and the Germans in British Children's Fiction from 1870 to the Present.* Tübingen: Stauggenburg Verlag

O'Sullivan, Emer (1995) 'Germany and Germans as Depicted in British Children's Literature from 1870 to the Present' in *Aspects and Issues in the History of Children's Literature*, Maria Nikolajeva (ed.). Westport, Connecticut: Greenwood, pp65-76

O'Sullivan, Emer (2000) 'Kulturelle Hybridität und Transfer. Black Britain in der (ins deutsche übersetzen) Kinder- und Jugendliteratur' in *Konfigurationen des Fremden in der Kinder- und Jugendliteratur Nach 1945*, Ulrich Nassen, Gina Weinkauff (eds.). Munich: Iudicum Verlag, pp75-93

Pageaux, Daniel-Henri (1989) 'De l'Imagerie culturelle à l'imaginaire' in *Précis de Littérature Comparée*, Pierre Brunel, Yves Chevrel (eds.) Paris: Presses Universitaires de France, pp133-161

Perrot, Jean (1998) 'A 'Little Tour' of the USA in Contemporary French Children's Literature' in *The Lion and the Unicorn,* 22, 1, January, pp71-91

Politou-Marmarinou, Eleni (1981) I Singritiki Filologia: Choros, Skopos ke Methodi Erevnas. Athens: Kardamitsa,

Pratt, Linda & Beaty, Janice J. (1990) *Transcultural Children's Literature.* Upper Saddle Hill, NJ: Prentice Hall

Prawer, S. S. (1973) *Comparative Literary Studies: An Introduction.* London: Duckworth

Renan, Ernest (1990) 'What is a Nation?' in *Nation and Narration*, Homi K. Bhabha (ed.). London and New York: Routledge, pp8-22

Rönnqvist, Lilian (2002) 'Secondary-level EFL: Melina Marchetta's *Looking for Alibrandi*' in *Children's Literature as Communication: The CHiLPA Project*, Roger. D. Sell (ed.). Amsterdam and Philadelphia: John Benjamins, pp315-331

Rutschmann, Verena (2000) 'Figuren des Fremden in der Schweizer Kinder- und Jugendliteratur Nach 1945', in *Konfiguationen des Fremden in der Kinder- und Jugenliteratur Nach 1945*, Ulrich Nassen, Gina Weinkauff (eds.). Munich: Indicum, pp21-37

Sarup, Madan (1996) *Identity, Culture and the Postmodern World.* Edinburgh: Edinburgh University Press

Siaflekis, Z. I. (1984) 'Singritiki Filologia ke Kinoniologia tis Logotechnias (Provlimata Methodou ke Erminias tou Logotechnikou kimenou)', in *Filologia* 8, pp18-30

Spiering, Menno (1992) *Englishness: Foreigners and Images of National Identity in Postwar Literature.* Amsterdam: Rodopi

Stephens, John (1997) 'Images of Australian Society in Australian Children's Literature' in *Gunpowder and Sealing-Wax: Nationhood in Children's Literature*, A. L. Lucas (ed.). Leicester: Troubador, pp15-24

Totosy de Zepetnek, Steven (1999) 'From Comparative Literature Today Toward Comparative Cultural Studies' in *CLCWeb: Comparative Literature and Culture: A WWWeb Journal*, (September 1999).
[Available at: http://clcwebjournal.lib.purdue.edu/clcweb99-3/totosy99.html] (accessed 23/10/2002)

Webb, Jean (ed.) (2000) *Text, Culture and National Identity in Children's Literature.* Helsinki: Nordinfo

Wellek, René & Warren, Austin (1956) *Theory of Literature.* 3rd edition. London: Harcourt Brace & Company

Williams, Sandra (2003) 'Constructing a National Identity through the *Adventures of a Nepali Frog*' in *Bookbird,* 41, 3, pp36-39

Yenika-Agbaw, Vivian (1998) 'Images of West Africa in Children's Books: Replacing Old Stereotypes with New Ones' in *The New Advocate,* 11, 3, Summer, pp203-218

Note

The background research for this paper was conducted under a research fellowship at the International Youth Library in Munich (IJB). I would like to thank the Director and staff of the library for all their help and support during my stay.

Children's Literature in Translation from East to West

Gabriele Thomson-Wohlgemuth

This essay discusses the social issues related to the translation of children's literature and contrasts the treatment of children's literature under the East German regime with the treatment of translation in the west today. There is a general assumption that western society has a more enlightened and liberal attitude whereas former Eastern Bloc societies tended to be more repressive (e.g. if one compares the political systems in east and west). This certainly appears to be true in terms of freedom of the press and the general freedom of expression but this is not the whole story. There are social factors at work in the west as much as in the east, and these assumptions may not be as clear cut in all matters related to freedom of expression and publication. Different cultures handle their texts differently in translation, be it the status that they attach to translated texts within in their culture or be it their reasons for selecting texts (see Toury's concept of norms, 1995). The translation of children's literature in particular sheds light on the social attitudes prevalent in a culture, consequently, 'the esteem in which a work of [children's] literature is held can also always be judged by the care and consideration its translation receives' (Kicherer as quoted in Osberghaus, 1994: 12, *my translation*). In its broadest sense this reveals the attitudes of a society towards not only the translated text but also the intended reader of the text. The German Democratic Republic (GDR) was no exception to the rule about the asymmetry of the relationship between the adults, who produce and buy the books, and the children, the intended readers. In the GDR this relationship was embodied in political doctrine whereby the objective of literature, whether indigenous or translated, was to create a new type of personality that would fit optimally into a socialist society. In contrast, western society is primarily concerned with commercial considerations before educational aspects. These issues will be explored in terms of the translation of the texts, the cultural aspects, the publishing policies and the status of translation.

Handling of translated texts

It does not come as a surprise that the content of East German books had to match the ideological and moral maxims of the state and, as a result, was vigilantly monitored. For a translation to be acceptable, certain notions had to be eliminated from foreign originals which were regarded as unacceptable for children, such as expressions of sentimentalism and 'kitsch', which were considered as characteristic of bourgeois societies, as well as passages deemed too violent or erotic. Other highly sensitive features which were omitted were those concerning religion, racism and colonial attitudes. So for instance the East German censorship files show that the two books *Pippi*

Longstocking and *Doctor Dolittle* had a complicated publishing history because of 'improper depiction of black people' (DR1/2253 and DR1/2275a, *my translation*). Extended negotiations with Lindgren and Lofting's son eventually resulted in deletions of several chapters from each book. As stated above, adjustments – be they justified or not – would be expected in a totalitarian state. What however is the situation in western countries?

Western societies as much as any other society have an interest in passing their value systems to the future generation. This concern becomes clear when examining translations performed and welcomed in these societies. Particularly during the decades between 1950 and 1970, a petty-bourgeois approach is discernible, cutting from translated texts what was not deemed appropriate to the existing moral value system. There we see, for example, the West German Pippi Longstocking changing her mind, after her first impulse to give pistols to her friends Annika and Tommy, lecturing them that 'they were nothing for children' (Paul, 1996: 16, *my translation*); or we experience some western nations shying away from too graphic expressions of bodily excretion – Astrid Lindgren herself reports that a chapter in one of her books has repeatedly been censored because of a scene in which one girl says to another 'you would not be able to stuff your nose full of peas because your nose is already full of snot' (1969: 98, *my translation*).

Other taboo areas, where well-meaning adults still tend to overprotect children in translations of children's books, deal with violence, eroticism and religion. The USA is particularly cautious in this area because it is a melting pot of a number of races and religions all of whom have to be accommodated. This has resulted in a policy of generally flattening stories, deleting any seemingly offensive elements from the texts and transforming them into sanitised, universal tales. The American educational establishment seems to seek to instil into children a certain kind of moral stability and purity combined with a conscious attitude of political correctness. So, for instance, Wally de Doncker's children's picture book *Ahum* has not yet been published in the USA, because it illustrates a couple hugging lovingly in bed. De Doncker was told there 'was no way the last two pages would not be censured', which surprised him, because in his opinion 'the book is nothing more than a critical view of our society and a tribute to tenderness' (2003, personal communication). In a second example Glyn Jones speaks about his experiences when translating eleven of Andersen's fairy tales in the early 1990s (1992: 18-20). He states that the American editor had made corrections in several areas, that is, religion (cuts with expressions mentioning God, heaven, etc), disrespect (a mother duck's remark about the duckling's father was toned down), violence (descriptions considered to be too graphic were deleted), sex and references to certain parts of the body (for example while in the original the mermaid covers her hair and breast with sea foam, in the American version she only covers her head), racial sensitivities (Thumbelina receives wings from a fly no longer described as 'white'; black magic turns into 'bad' magic), style (Andersen's conversational style had been transformed into a formal literary style). Jones criticises these changes not only from an ethical point of view but also because he claims that, through these adjustments, his translation was turned into a colourless text, from which humour and specific flavour had disappeared.

However, other cultures and epochs are as guilty of text modifications 'for the good of the child'. To complete the picture, it should be added that text interference does not necessarily have to be restricted to omissions. Additions, explanations and embellishments may equally have pedagogical reasons and can give a different character to the text (see for example Christiane Jung, 1996).

Regrettably, it seems to be the case that more emphasis is placed on producing 'suitable' books for children than on the child's enjoyment of the text; that the didactic, moral, religious, ideological parts count more than the informative, therapeutic and entertaining. Why is it that adjustments are deemed necessary when a text is targeted at a new audience? Puurtinen gives three reasons: firstly, she claims, children's literature is governed by various changing principles (morale, ideology, religion, etc.) which determine what kind of literature children are provided with; secondly, children's books must appeal to the primary group, children, but also to adults who constitute the taste-setting authority and, ultimately, the buyers; thirdly, the child's limited reading abilities, experience of life and knowledge of the world must be taken into consideration (1994: 83). Particularly, this third point illustrates another argument, namely that not all text adjustments are based purely on pedagogical reasons. There is, of course, the question of how much 'otherness' children can accept in their books; what is the optimum number of explanations that can be added without overloading the text and risking the child's loss of interest? It has been, and still is, widely debated among scholars, how much of the foreign culture should be allowed to shine through and to what degree a text should be domesticated. In other words, the more a translator (or publisher) trusts their readers to cope with difficult expressions and unfamiliar concepts, the more they will favour closeness to the source text and enable the children to learn about foreign cultures and to widen their knowledge.

What is sameness/otherness and how does it fare in translation?

Being part of the Eastern Bloc, East Germany felt itself closer to its brother nations than to the western capitalist systems. This explains why the vast majority of East German children's literature translations stems from socialist countries, with Soviet literature constituting the main proportion of translated literature. Russian was the main foreign language taught at school, and everybody was familiar with Russian history and culture. Within this structure, translations from western countries played a minor role, in that fewer books were translated. This was mostly based on the different ideology which was not considered compatible with socialism. Hence, western books were generally chosen for the purpose of portraying capitalism as an evil, defective, corrupt social system. This, in turn, was to support the socialist cause by giving evidence of the strength and worthiness of socialism. What happened in the socialist confederation is the perfectly natural and understandable phenomenon of countries aligning themselves with like-minded societies, within which language, literature and communication plays a vital role.

It is easier to translate texts between similar cultures than those which are vastly different. This is because the languages of related cultures have similar historical roots and language patterns. Another reason is the fact that a country's children's literature, representative of its cultural background, is determined by pedagogical, moral and political values, and for children to understand and process these values, they need to be equated with familiar ideas. Thus, similar concepts in the literature of source language and target language will help the transposition process. As has become evident in the case of Eastern Bloc countries, there are different, closely-linked, geographical regions which facilitate or hinder the contribution that children's literature can make to international understanding by their influence on the distribution paths of translated children's books. 'Children's literature regions' (Klingberg, 1973: 90 & 1978: 89), that is a group of countries characterised by a common pattern regarding the source languages of published translations, arise mainly as a result of historical ties and they will, to a large degree, show similar socio-cultural structures. Within each region, the impact of children's books from different languages shows roughly the same pattern and books in certain languages are translated more often than books in other languages. Since therefore translations represent cultural transfers, attempting to render the culture-specific details of the target language, the probability is high that a translator or editor will carry out more adjustments in the case of major cultural differences between source and target text.

A number of studies have been undertaken to trace the flow of literature, in order to determine which countries enjoy closely-affiliated relationships. Findings have demonstrated that Scandinavia, Germany and Austria belong to the same geographical children's literature region (see Furuland, 1978; Shine, 1978); so do Asiatic countries; the English-speaking countries too have between themselves a regular exchange of their respective literatures, and the Spanish and French regions also form a close connection.

A revealing study was conducted by Rutschmann (1996: 12-22), investigating the different language areas within the Swiss confederation. Her analysis disclosed that the German, Italian and French area mainly exchanged literature with neighbouring countries of the same language whilst between one another there was hardly any cultural exchange at all. Another significant aspect of Rutschmann's discoveries is the existence of different notions of childhood in each Swiss language area and how this is expressed in children's literature. This underscores my findings about the Eastern Bloc countries who share the same image of the child which, however, differs greatly from that of other cultures (for example in the GDR children were seen as equal partners in the class struggle).

According to the degree of cultural closeness or alternatively the degree of foreignness, different considerations will play a role and different processes will come into play. If cultural differences are too big and are thought impossible to overcome, the result will be that a book is not translated at all. In the event of less dominant cultural specifics (which is the case with the majority of translations), it is up to publishers to decide, if and when to withhold information or whether to make available the culture-specific elements to the readers. This harks back to the afore-mentioned issue of how much otherness a translator/publisher expects children to be able to cope with, all of which goes to show that text alterations may have not only pedagogical/ideological motives but may arise through a certain cultural distance.

Publishing policies, status of translated texts

In many cases, publishers encounter additional expenditure, should they want to publish a foreign book. Royalties may have to be purchased and naturally the translator also needs to be paid. Hence, publishers are in the predicament of deciding whether a book will find sufficient buyers to bring in profit and whether it is therefore worthwhile commissioning the translation. Conversely, the GDR commonly found itself in the situation where the readership was eager for any translated book; however, the problem was obtaining the finance and resources to publish the book in the first place. The East German Mark was not convertible in western markets and, thus, the country was notoriously short of western currency. As a result, this made books from the Eastern Bloc cheaper and easier to translate and produce, whereas economic constraints were much more of a determining factor in the translation of books from the west. Consequently, publishers sought to achieve co-productions or to sell part of the edition into the west.

In a competitive economy, however, saleability and profit maximisation prevail and every decision has to balance production costs against estimated consumer demand. In contrast to socialist countries, alternative entertainment opportunities in the west are many and the chances that a book remains on the shelf are consequently greater. Although, in the case of translated books, co-productions aid in reducing production costs, publishers have to watch carefully the market, their competitors and their budget.

Tying in with market constraints, the phenomenon of the pervasiveness of the English language, having become the global *lingua franca*, has been observed during the past two decades. What are the implications of this development for translation in general and translated children's literature in particular? This pervasiveness of English accounts for the low status of translated foreign fiction in English-speaking countries; hence, the majority of publishers in these countries hesitate to commit themselves financially to the translation of foreign literature. Simultaneously, an atmosphere of ignorance towards other cultures and societies is prevalent. The situation in smaller language areas however is quite the opposite. People living in such communities are highly aware of the English culture and, generally, fiction originating from English-speaking nations does not take long to be translated. Another observation is that English sets the standards of literary tradition to which fiction from different literary regions tends to adhere. This clearly makes English a strong, self-sufficient language which does not depend on translation from other literatures. As a corollary, translated works maintain a peripheral position. A further characteristic of translated literature in English-speaking countries is its strong orientation towards the target text culture (see Even-Zohar, 1987).

There is plentiful evidence for these findings. For decades, the Anglo-American market has dominated children's literature translation. Whereas Britain and America depend mainly on their combined national literatures and hardly translate anything, the proportion of translation in other European, that is lesser-used language countries is fairly high.

For the year 1986, Jobe reported that 50% of Swedish titles were translations, of which 75% were imported from Anglo-American sources; figures in the opposite direction show only 2,7% of original Swedish titles were translated into US editions and 7,5% into British ones (1987: 8). In 1987, there were 450 translations per 10 million citizens in Germany from Anglo-American sources alone, 4 per 10 million from German into the UK and none into America (Birkenhauer, 1989: 430). More recent research demonstrates a further decline of translations into English-speaking countries. Klaus Flugge made public this sorry state from the other side of the fence (1994: 19; 1993: 15). Speaking both as a German national and as the head of a British publishing house for children, he distinguished the following reasons for this state of affairs, namely: problems linked with the declining sales of hardback books; cuts in public spending; reluctance of many parents and teachers to spend time over a book with children which results in the production of books that can be enjoyed and understood by children on their own; drop in sales of more demanding and sophisticated books; insufficient quantity of good children's literature in British bookshops, compared to other European countries; a certain fear in Britons of their feelings and their dislike of anything unfamiliar and carrying the label of 'problem book with a difficult subject'. Buss added to this list the observations that Britain has become more 'chauvinistic', 'culturally exclusive' and 'less eager for her children to learn other languages' (1994: 11).

Equally, there is a trend in America to distinguish itself from British culture, a notion underlined by Nel's recent article about the 'translation' of *Harry Potter* into American English. This translation constitutes a distinct domestication of the text by erasing from it British culture-specific details. Having received criticism for contributing to the 'dumb[ing] down of US society', the editor defended his act as wanting 'to make sure that an American kid reading the book would have the same literary experience that a British kid would have' (2000: 261). However, such acts tend to be regarded as American arrogance, whereby the economic imperative of selling to the vast American market, engineered by multinational capitalism, 'gives US publishers the belief that they have license to Americanize British texts' (p272).

Since this asymmetric development has manifested itself globally over the last decades and there is no sign of a reversal of this one-way trade, some importance should be attached to it. Not only does it mean that Europe is flooded with 'English' literature and, simultaneously, with 'English' culture and the 'English' way of thinking; conversely, the English-speaking countries do not gain any of the richness in literatures from cultures other than their own.

Faced with such grim facts, it would appear that the asymmetric power relationship between adult and child, in translated children's literature, has wider repercussions than originally assumed. It appears that the west is mirroring the situation created by repressive Eastern Bloc countries, that is selection of books, changes to the text and the power relationship towards the readers, but for different reasons.

Theorists have attempted to find explanations for this kind of development and have formulated the concept of polysystems, later refined by Shavit for the field of children's literature (1981: 171-177). The interrelationship between different systems within a culture and between cultures has been studied, and translated children's literature can been assigned a floating position within the structure for each country, albeit with a tendency to remain on the periphery. As expected, depending on the status of translation within the culture, more or less translation from foreign cultures takes place. In the case of the GDR, translation changed its position within the polysystem in line with political changes in the country, that is in the early stages of the country, translated literature from the Union of Socialist Soviet Republics (USSR) played a central role, being decisive in shaping the country's notion of children's literature and influencing East Germany's future 'home-grown' production. Once indigenous GDR writing had been established, translations (and western translations even more so) fell back to assume a peripheral role. The same polysystemic structures show the increasingly marginalized position of translated literature in Britain and America and a corresponding increase in translation of English literature into non-English-speaking countries. This indicates that within the 'European macro-polysystem' (Even-Zohar, 1987: 112) a gradual restructuring in cultural concepts is taking place. With the breakdown of the Eastern Bloc this has accelerated the changes, as these countries try to align themselves with western culture and, in so doing, further contribute to the shift.

Hence, while it is true that adults have firm ideas about the literature with which they want their children to grow up and, thus, adjust it because of the need to educate children towards the 'right' cultural and linguistic values; and while it is true that the requirement of faithfulness to the original is outweighed by other constraints (market considerations etc.), it would seem that even higher mechanisms at present dominate the makeup of the global polysystem. It is evident that social and political trends are reflected in literary texts – indeed, observation of events in children's literature translations during the past decades indicates a gradual drift toward a uniform, bland, non-pluralistic super-culture dominated by western economic and social policies.

Bibliography

Birkenhauer, Klaus (1989) 'Buch-Binnenmarkt: Bis an die Sprachbarrieren, aber Keinen Schritt Weiter' in *Börsenblatt für den Deutschen Buchhandel,* 10, pp430-31

Buss, Robin (1994) 'Rates of Exchange' in *Times Educational Supplement*, 25 March, p11

Even-Zohar, Itamar (1987) 'The Position of Translated Literature Within the Literary Polysystem' in *Indian Journal of Applied Linguistics,* 13, pp107-115

Flugge, Klaus (1993) 'Lost Opportunities. We are Neglecting Powerful Fiction from Abroad' in *Times Educational Supplement*, 2 April, p15

Flugge, Klaus (1994) 'Crossing the Divide' in *The Bookseller*, 8 April, pp18-19

Furuland, Lars (1978) 'Sweden and the International Children's Book Market: History and Present Situation' in *Children's Books in Translation. The Situation and the Problems.* Göte Klingberg, Mary Ørvig, Stuart Amor (eds.) Stockholm: Almqvist & Wiksell International, pp60-75

Jobe, Ronald (1987) 'Translation for Young People: an Endangered Species?' in *Bookbird,* 25,1, pp8-9

Jones, Glyn (1992) 'HC and PC' in *Professional Translator & Interpreter* , 3, pp18-20

Jung, Christiane (1996) 'Tea-time oder Kaffee und Kuchen? Von den Schwierigkeiten des Übersetzens' in *Bulletin Jugend und Literatur,* 2, pp13-20

Klingberg, Göte (1973) *Kinder -und Jugendliteraturforschung. Eine Einführung*. Graz: Hermann Böhlaus Nachf.

Klingberg, Göte (1978) 'The Different Aspects of Research into the Translation of Children's Books and its Practical Application' in *Children's Books in Translation. The Situation and the Problems*, Göte Klingberg, Mary Ørvig, Stuart Amor (eds.). Stockholm: Almqvist & Wiksell International, pp84-89

Lindgren, Astrid (1969) 'Traduire des Livres d'enfant – est-ce possible?' in *Babel*, pp98-100

Nel, Philip (2000) 'You Say 'Jelly', I Say 'Jell-O'? Harry Potter and the Transfiguration of Language' in *The Ivory Tower and Harry Potter*, Lana Whited. Missouri: University of Missouri Press, pp261-284

Osberghaus, Monika (1994) 'Übersetzen ist eine Lebensform. Ein Porträt der Übersetzerin Birgitta Kicherer' in *Bulletin Jugend und Literatur,* 10, pp12-16

Paul, Reimar (1996) 'Pippi Langstrumpf an der Leine. Wie der Kinder-Klassiker aus Schweden für Brave Deutsche Kinder Umgeschrieben Wurde'. in *Süddeutsche Zeitung*, 7/8, p16

Puurtinen, Tiina (1994) 'Dynamic Style as a Parameter of Acceptability in Translated Children's Books' in *Translation Studies. An Interdiscipline*, Mary Snell-Hornby. Amsterdam: John Benjamins, pp83-90

Rutschmann, Verena (1996) 'Kinderliterarisches Übersetzen und Interkultureller Austausch' in *Zum Übersetzen von Kinder- und Jugendliteratur*, Walter Lenschen. Lausanne: Travaux du Centre de Traduction Littéraire, pp6-22

Shavit, Zohar (1981) 'Translation of Children's Literature as a Function of Its Position in the Literary Polysystem' in *Poetics Today,* 2, 4, pp171-179

Shine, Norman (1978) 'The Translation of Children's Literature: a Case of English Children's Books Written Between 1800 and 1900 and at Some Point in Time Translated into Danish' in *Children's Books in Translation. The Situation and the Problems*, Göte Klingberg, Mary Ørvig, Stuart Amor (eds.). Stockholm: Almqvist & Wiksell International, pp113-129

Thomson-Wohlgemuth, Gaby (2003) 'Publication History of *Ahum.*' E-mail to Wally De Doncker, 14 August.

Toury, Gideon (1995) *Descriptive Translation Studies and Beyond.* Amsterdam & Philadelphia: John Benjamins

Censorship Files

Publisher's statement. File DR1/2253. 5 June 1967.

Publisher's statement. File DR1/2275a. 18 June 1974.

About the Contributors

Perry Nodelman teaches children's literature courses as a Professor of English at the University of Winnipeg, Winnipeg, Manitoba, Canada. He is the author of children's and young adult novels as well as about a hundred articles and two books about children's literature: *Words About Pictures: the Narrative Art of Children's Picture Books* (University of Georgia Press) and, in collaboration with Mavis Reimer, the third edition of *The Pleasures of Children's Literature* (Allyn & Bacon). In 2005, he will become Editor of *CCL/LCJ*, the Canadian Children's Literature journal.

Peter Hunt was the first specialist in Children's Literature to be appointed as full Professor in a British University English Department. He has published 16 books [among which are: *Criticism, Theory, & Children's Literature* (1991), *An Introduction to Children's Literature* (1994), and *Children's Literature: A Guide* (2001)] and over 200 articles on the subject, and 6 books for the young. He researches and teaches at Cardiff University, in Wales.

Rebecca Rabinowitz has a Bachelor's degree from Wesleyan University and a Master's Degree from the Center for the Study of Children's Literature at Simmons College, where she was a Virginia Haviland Scholar. She writes children's literature criticism and reviews for several journals, including *Kirkus Reviews*. She lives in Cambridge, Massachusetts.

Vanessa Joosen was born in 1977 in Antwerp, Belgium, where she is still living. She has a Master's Degree in English and German Literature from the University of Antwerp and a Master's Degree in Children's Literature from the University of Surrey, Roehampton. She has worked as a book reviewer for *Achuka* and *Leesidee Jeugdliteratuur* and is part of the board of I.B.B.Y. Flanders. In 2003 she received a four-year FWO scholarship from the Belgian government to start a PhD in Children's Literature. Her research interests are: young adult fiction, fairytale retellings, criticism on children's literature and translation.

Karen Sands-O'Connor is Assistant Professor at Buffalo State College in Buffalo, New York, where she teaches children's and young adult literature, twentieth century British literature, and literary criticism. She has recently published in *Diana Wynne Jones: An Exciting and Exacting Wisdom* published by Peter Lang and *Utopias and Dystopias for Children* from Routledge. Her work has increasingly focused on the role that the non-English character plays in British children's literature, and ranges from an examination of the Welsh origins of the city of London to contemporary young adult literature about racism in Britain.

Laura Atkins worked for almost ten years in the children's publishing industry in the United States of America, the last two of which she spent as an editor of multicultural picture books at Lee & Low Books in New York City. Books on which she has worked have won a variety of honours, including the Coretta Scott King Award and a Bank Street Book of the Year Award. She completed her M.A. in Children's Literature at the University of Surrey, Roehampton, and is now pursuing a PhD at the same university with a focus on multicultural children's literature and the publishing process.

Ann Alston is currently studying for a PhD at Cardiff University. Her research is concerned with perceived changes in family and family structure in Western society and their relation to children's literature over the last two hundred years. Previous publications include an article on the Father in the *Swallows and Amazons* series, and a forthcoming article on food in children's literature. This essay originates from part of the third chapter of her PhD dissertation which looks at representations of the house and home in children's literature and considers the somewhat mythological status that the home has acquired.

David Rudd is a senior lecturer in the Department of Cultural & Creative Studies at Bolton Institute, Lancashire, where he teaches courses on education, research methods, and literature, including children's literature. Aside from some 65 articles on the latter, he has written books on Roald Dahl (*A Communication Studies Approach to Children's Literature*, 1992) and Enid Blyton (*Enid Blyton and the Mystery of Children's Literature*, 2000). Recent works have been on *Rupert Bear* and Deleuze, Lacan and the *Faraway Tree*, Sinclair's *Holiday House*, and 'The Conditions of Possibility of Children's Literature' for the new edition of the *International Companion Encyclopedia of Children's Literature*.

Katrien Vloeberghs is writing a PhD (for which she received a FWO scholarship from the Belgian government) on the image and discourse of the child in literary modernism, recent theory and contemporary children's and youth literature. She is teaching Masters courses at the University of Antwerp on various topics in children's literature: (post)modernist characteristics of children's literature, the paradigm of initiation in YA literature, the construction and transformation of the enlightened and the romantic concept of child and childhood, and the representation of the holocaust in contemporary children's literature. She has published articles on the image of the child and the topic of youth in literature for children and adults, and reviews children's books on a regular basis in several publications.

Virginie Douglas teaches in the department of English at Rouen University (France). Her PhD dissertation analysed the place of subversion in contemporary British fantasy for children (La Subversion dans la Fiction Non-réaliste Contemporaine pour la Jeunesse au Royaume-Uni [1945-

95]). She has published several articles in France on contemporary children's novels, particularly on narration, its specificity and its new trends in texts produced for young readers. She is currently writing some entries for Oxford University Press's forthcoming *Encyclopedia of Children's Literature.*

Maiko Miyoshi studied English Literature in Japan and completed an MA in Children's Literature at the University of Surrey, Roehampton. Her interests in 'writing characters' in children's literature has been growing since her MA dissertation. She continues to investigate the topic as a research student at Roehampton, particularly the representation of writing as an act, and various writing accounts by characters in children's fiction.

Alison Waller is a doctoral student at Nottingham Trent University and her thesis examines representations of adolescence in young adult fantastic realism. Her focus is the cultural development of this genre and its interactions with other discourses of the teenager. Aspects that she has presented at conferences include ghost novels, fantasy worlds, metamorphosis and theories of adolescence. Her other interests include work on fantasy more generally, children's and young adult literature theory, and creative writing. She has written an article on Margaret Mahy's use of witchcraft themes ('Solid all the Way Through: Margaret Mahy's Ordinary Witches', to be published in *Children's Literature in Education,* 35, 1, Spring 2004) and a critical recollection of the pleasures of reading teenage fiction ('*Fade* and the Lone Teenager: Young Adult Fantastic Realism Shaping Modern Individualism' in *Children's Fantasy Fiction: Debates for the 21st Century*, edited by Nickianne Moody and Clare Horrocks).

Dominique Sandis is currently a full-time PhD student in Children's Literature at the National Centre for Research in Children's Literature (University of Surrey, Roehampton). She has a Bachelor's Degree in Applied Languages from the University of Brighton and an M.A. in Children's Literature from the University of Reading up her sleeve. Her main focus is on the construction of nation and identity in children's and young adult literature. Her articles and other work on children's literature have appeared in British, American, German and Greek publications.

Gabriele Thomson-Wohlgemuth holds an M A in Translation Studies and is at present writing a PhD thesis in the area of translation of children's literature. Her publications focus on indigenous East German children's and youth literature, translation of English children's books in the former East Germany as well as on general issues regarding translation, the publishing industry and cultural/literary politics in the German Democratic Republic.